Leavenworth Papers

No. 6

Soviet Night Operations in World War II

by Major Claude R. Sasso

Combat Studies Institute
U.S. Army Command and General Staff College
Fort Leavenworth, Kansas 66027

December 1982

Contents

Maps v

Preface vii

Introduction ix

Soviet Night Operations 1

Conclusion 33

Appendix. Table of Soviet Night Operations 41

Notes 45

Bibliography 53

Maps

1. Moscow Counteroffensive and Airborne Drops 4
2. Battle of Stalingrad 7
3. Day and Night Attacks of the Soviet 5th Guards
   Tank Army at Kharkov 8
4. Battle of the Dnieper/Airborne Insertion 10
5. Battles of Zaporozh'e and Kiev 12
6. Korsun-Shevchenkovsky Operation 15
7. Crimean Offensive 17
8. Byelorussian Campaign 19
9. Advance to the Oder 20
10. The Battle of Berlin 22
11. The Manchurian Campaign 27

Preface

Clausewitz in his classic *On War* aptly described the "fog of war" in his discussion of "friction," the difference between plans and reality that renders impossible an examination of war as an orderly, rational process. Observed Clausewitz, "Everything in war is very simple, but the simplest thing is difficult." The knowledge of war's friction—its confusion, unpredictability, and chaos; the "influence of an infinity of petty circumstances"—daily confronts the military planner and leader. At no time is the fog of war more pronounced than at night. Night operations have long posed an obstacle and a challenge for soldiers. Commanders throughout history have recognized the military advantages afforded by darkness; they have also been painfully aware of the enormous difficulties attendant upon launching troops into the trap of night. Thus, while many military leaders of the past have embraced the night and sought to use it to their advantage, many more have avoided the consideration and use of night operations.

Modern armies seeking to mitigate the devastating effects of firepower and the increasingly vicious nature of combat in the twentieth century have found cause to consider or reconsider the feasibility of night operations. In no army has this tendency been clearer than in the Soviet Army, especially during its struggle for survival in World War II. Driven by desperation and necessity, the Red Army launched nocturnal offensives as a hedge against the huge losses incurred in daytime fighting and as a means of applying unrelenting pressure on an overextended German Army. Advising that "night offensives can be successful only in conditions of thorough preparation and careful organization," the Field Regulations of 1942 reflected initial Soviet caution in giving battle after dark. But as the Soviet Army's struggle for survival evolved into a successful struggle for dominance over the German Army, Soviet night operations matured. The Field Regulations of 1944 echoed that growing confidence: "Under present day conditions tactical actions at night are usual occurrences. The darkness of night (or fog) favors surprise to the maximum degree and lessens losses from fire." Pursuant to the regulation, night operations grew in number, boldness, and scale. In the final Soviet action of World War II, the Manchurian campaign in August 1945, a strategic offensive with more than a million soldiers, was launched shortly after midnight, in many sectors during torrential rains.

The Soviet World War II experience does not stand in isolation. As Major Sasso points out in the introduction to this *Leavenworth Paper*, the czarist forerunner of the Red Army demonstrated a "predilection for night operations." And as specialists in the field are fully aware, Soviet regulations before the outbreak of war in 1939 recognized that "night operations will be common under modern warfare conditions to exploit surprise, reduce losses, and disorganize the enemy." Soviet writings in the postwar years have continued to emphasize that belief in the utility of night operations, particularly in an offensive role. That emphasis underscores the likelihood of heavy Soviet reliance on the cover of night, especially in the initial phases of combat. Prudence dictates that potential adversaries of the Soviet Army develop an understanding of Soviet night operations and make preparations to cope with them. An excellent place to begin is with a study of the nature of Soviet night combat in World War II, one of the major focuses of study and inspiration for today's Soviet officer. This *Leavenworth Paper* provides an introductory survey of that oft-overlooked Soviet experience. We hope that it will further a better understanding of the essence of Soviet night combat in its wartime context.

Because the friction of war will persist and night combat will continue to exemplify that friction, one must follow the advice that Clausewitz offered to those who must endure the fog of war: amass experience. "Only the experienced officer will make the right decision in major or minor matters—at every pulsebeat of war. Practice and experience dictate the answer: this is possible, that is not." This study of one facet of Soviet operations in World War II offers at least vicarious experience to the officer who reads it and ponders its meaning and implications.

Lieutenant Colonel David M. Glantz
Curriculum Supervisor
Combat Studies Institute

Introduction

Surprise is a vital ingredient in conducting successful warfare. As early as 500 B.C., the Chinese general Sun Tzu recognized this simple fact in his oft-quoted treatise on the art of war. Throughout history, commanders have employed the darkness of night to gain surprise and to grasp the initiative from the hands of the enemy. Yet, while night operations have progressed from the nocturnal marches of Joshua and the exploits of Judas Maccabeus in biblical times to the more recent firefights in Vietnam and Afghanistan, problems involving special night training, control, and manpower have more often than not dissuaded commanders from attempting large-scale operations in the dark. Night combat has frequently been the recourse of the inferior military force or, as in World War II, of the army seeking either to find some respite from air power or to reduce casualties in the face of great firepower. Still, despite the difficulties associated with conducting military operations at night, military planners and leaders cannot escape one salient fact: darkness is "a double-edged weapon," and like terrain, "it favors the one who best uses it and hinders the one who does not."[1]

Since their conflict with the Ottoman Turks in 1877—78, the Russians have shown both a predilection for night operations and considerable skill in conducting them.[2] The Russo-Japanese War (1904—5) witnessed no fewer than 106 night attacks of company size or larger, as both sides relied on night to shield them from the increased lethality of firepower.[3] In World War I, the Russians conducted large-scale assaults at night with as many as eighteen waves of infantry. The mass attacks of 1914—15 often failed because of poor planning, but even the Germans acknowledged that the war proved Russian night training had been superior to their own.[4] During the civil war that engulfed Russia at war's end, the Red Army successfully capped its Crimean offensive by capturing the difficult fortifications on the isthmus of Perekop during a night attack conducted by troops wading across the icy waters of Sivash Bay, while the defenders faced a frontal assault.

During World War II, the Soviets effectively exploited darkness in a variety of operations from withdrawal to pursuit. As the war dragged on, the Red Army relied increasingly on night operations and so refined its abilities that it was able to progress from limited tactical missions by relatively small units to front-level operations by armies with complex coordination and control. Today Soviet military writers frequently discuss night operations, as they do all operations, with reference to their experiences in the Second World War. They appear convinced, as one Soviet general and historian has noted, that their "troops should be equally capable of operating both during the day and at night" and that night operations have an "urgent significance in modern warfare."[5]

This study began as an attempt to shed light on the numerous and, in the West, rarely scrutinized Soviet night operations of World War II. The dearth of studies can be traced to the problem of source material. After the war, former high-ranking German officers addressed night combat on the Eastern Front as a separate subject in their writings, but their efforts tended to concentrate on the years 1941 and 1942, with little discussion of the later years of the war, when Soviet operations matured, and with no discussion whatsoever of night operations during the fateful year 1945. Another problem for historians in the decades immediately after the war was the comparative dearth of translated Soviet analysis and documentation on this subject, in contrast to the multitude of German battle accounts available to Western scholars. During the past two decades, however, the Soviets have written profusely on their experiences in the war. This study takes advantage of these Soviet writings as well as German and other available sources. From what I have extracted from these sources, I have endeavored to write an introduction to Soviet night operations during the war.

Major Claude R. Sasso
Professor of Military Science
University of California, Los Angeles

Soviet Night Operations: Evolution and Growth in World War II

The Germans launched their three-pronged blitzkrieg against the Soviet Union on 22 June 1941. Caught unprepared, the Soviets experienced a series of reverses, as German armor surrounded many large Russian units and forced others to withdraw. Those that withdrew often did so at night, in double march columns. In one instance, recounted by General V. Kuznetsov, commander of the Soviet 21st Army,* the Russians moved units from the Parichi-Mozyr sector of the Southwestern Front to hastily established defensive positions on the west side of the Dnieper, 120 kilometers to the rear. The withdrawal required three nights of marching. During the day, troops and trains were concealed in towns and wooded areas (with Soviet aircraft checking the extent of concealment every morning at dawn). The troops completed this series of night marches without the loss of a vehicle or machine gun. Kuznetsov attributed this remarkable feat to enforced discipline and thorough day-to-day preparation:

> In each regiment one organized a group of officers and privates, the missions of which were: to reconnoiter the march route . . . to lay out, where necessary, a cross country route of march; to station posts for traffic regulation; to plan in the area of the day halt lines for security at the halt; to select concealed places for bivouacs. In addition to this, from the makeup of the staffs of the troops of combined arms one assigned officers to see that the troops observed in a strict manner all the rules of night march.[6]

The discipline and organization that proved so effective in the foregoing example were not always replicated in Soviet night marches early in the war. During the first stage of the conflict (22 June 1941—19 November 1942), the Russians did not always permit or undertake timely withdrawals. Consequently, many Soviet units found themselves encircled. To break out, they launched surprise attacks, often at night. At Smolensk, the tactic succeeded: fierce Soviet counterattacks to the south extricated five divisions on the night of 23 July 1941 and elements of three more the next day.[7] In other areas, however, similar operations did not fare as well. Many of the Red

---

*Ed. note: Beginning with this issue of *Leavenworth Papers*, we have simplified unit designations for the convenience of our readers.

Army's desperate efforts to break out at night amounted to "massed infantry rushes," sometimes along roads, but more frequently across open or hindering terrain.[8] At Vyazma, for example, four encircled Soviet armies under General M. Lukin failed to break out in three columns to the north. An attempt to break out to the east over swampy terrain nearly succeeded, but the Germans quickly closed the gap. Finally, after six days and nights, Lukin broke his forces down into separate groups and ordered them to fight their way out to the south, after destroying their vehicles and horses. Only then were many of the soldiers able to extricate themselves from the German trap.[9]

A German view of these breakouts is enlightening:

> To succeed in their withdrawals the Russian command frequently sacrificed rear guards ruthlessly... the Russian civilian population was relentlessly put to work at night digging antitank ditches or building covering or dummy positions.
> In nearly all their disengagement movements the Russians were supported by tanks. The importance of mines as a modern means of combat for use at night had been recognized by the Russians at the very beginning of the war.[10]

In the Arctic, where the protection of the Murmansk lifeline was vital, the Soviets employed commando teams deep in the German rear. These commandos, specially trained at Byelomorsk in night raids, carried only essential items and operated methodically under "minutely detailed orders." As in other areas of the front, their attacks were broken off only when their casualties "amounted to many times the strength of the strong-point complements."[11] Even though the polar winter limited fighting in this area to a small scale, surprise attacks were common because the days remained dark.

Farther to the south, around Leningrad, the Russians countered the Germans' daytime gains with a succession of night counterattacks. Night attacks were also effective in the Moscow area during the frigid winter of 1941—42, especially after the arrival of eighteen fresh Siberian divisions. In late November, one of these divisions directed a night attack against the German 112th Infantry Division, operating south of Moscow and east of Uzlovaya. A part of General Heinz Guderian's 2d Panzer Group, the 112th had lost 500 men to frostbite. The severe cold prevented the Germans' machine guns from working, and to make matters worse, their 37-mm antitank guns proved ineffective against Soviet T-34 tanks. The attack came early in the night, when the 112th was in bivouac. A German account reveals the scene:

> About twenty tanks led the Siberian attack. The mere appearance by night of tanks in front of the lines of the 112th Division produced a severe shock. No means of defense were at hand for the time being. At that, any defenses would have had only a local effect at night. When the attacking Siberians now appeared behind the tanks, complete panic broke out. The elements of the 112th Division hit by the attack fell back many kilometers .... Special steps had to be taken to restore control of the situation.[13]

In this particular battle, the Russians did not immediately attempt to exploit their success beyond a few kilometers. The reasons for this are not clear. Perhaps the Siberian division had achieved its objectives when it halted. More significant, perhaps it felt constrained by doctrine that seemed to limit the scope of night missions. The basic 1936 Field Regulations, still in effect at the beginning of the war, recommended night attacks by battalions or even by regiments, but not by divisions unless the circumstances were exceptional. The draft 1940 Field Regulations were no less restrictive, stressing as they did the problems of control and limiting the depth of nighttime offensive operations.

The realities of war soon weakened the restraints of an inadequate doctrine. The first period of the war, as we have seen, pointed out the value of night attacks. This and the fact that the Germans had command of the air led the Russians to increase the scope and frequency of night operations. A special directive issued by the Military Council of the Western Front on 29 December 1941 stated:

> As of today commence extensive surprise nighttime operations. In the evening send out ambushes of small fighting detachments on the roads deep in the enemy positions. All nighttime attacks on population points are to be prepared for before nightfall. The troops are to be brought up to the jump-off position for an attack also before nightfall. Guides and submachine gunners are to be widely used.[14]

General Guenther Blumentritt, the chief of staff of the German 4th Army in front of Moscow, characterized the Russians as "night-happy" and noted that an excellent infantry division in the 4th Army was considered unreliable at night because it had suffered heavy losses to Soviet night attacks at Smolensk and later at the Desna River, before the Moscow campaign got underway. He maintained that the Russian activity at night forced the Germans to be equally active in order to measure up to the "Russian standards of night warfare."[15]

Russian sources also acknowledge the importance of night attacks in the counteroffensive against the Germans at Moscow. One such source records that the 320th and 323d Rifle Divisions, at 2400 on the night of 6—7 December 1941, launched an attack that played a key role in turning back the offensive of the 2d Panzer Group in the Tula region. Regimental and divisional ski troops advanced two kilometers, the average depth for a night attack in the first period of the war. In some isolated sectors, Russian troops penetrated to a depth of six or seven kilometers, a substantial distance, considering that, to achieve surprise, they attacked without an artillery preparation and, in most cases, without accompanying fires. As might be expected, the Soviets considered command and control their chief problem, not only because of the limited daylight hours available to orient troops on the terrain and to assign missions, but also because of a shortage of colored rockets and other signal devices. For these reasons, at least in the first stage of the war, the Soviets did not attempt complicated maneuvers by battalions or regiments at night, such as the calling up of second echelons or reserves.[16]

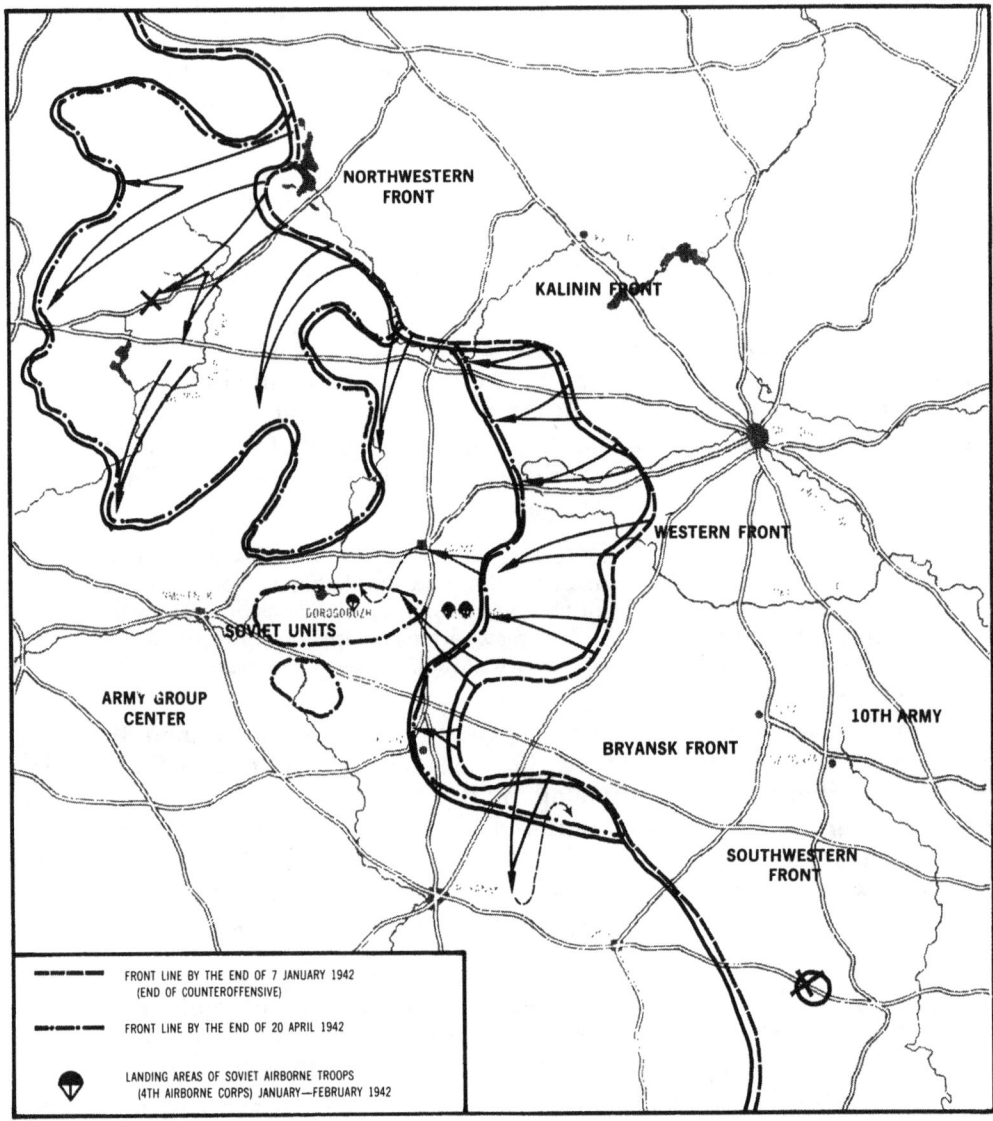

Map 1. Moscow Counteroffensive and Airborne Drops

No discussion of night operations during the Moscow counteroffensive would be complete without mention of a bold but less than successful undertaking during January and February 1942 in the area southwest of Vyazma. On 27 January, the Soviet 4th Airborne Corps began a series of night drops of paratroopers in the German rear. Forty civilian and twenty-two military aircraft, escorted by limited numbers of fighters and ground attack aviation, supported the landings. From the beginning, the operation did not go well. After six nights, only 2,100 men from the 10,000-man airborne corps had been dropped in. Because of bad weather and the pilots' inexperience with night navigation, most of these troops landed twenty kilometers south of the intended drop zone. Plans for five to six sorties each night did not take into account adverse weather conditions, aircraft failures, or combat losses. Also, the failure to conceal the buildup of troops at the airborne fields led to the closing of one of them by German bombers. The remaining two fields provided only two to three sorties per night. The paratroops that landed, however, did succeed in interdicting lines of communication in the German rear area for almost three weeks, in part because of their linkup with the 1st Guards Cavalry Corps on 6 February.

A second series of night landings occurred near Yukhnov between 17 and 23 February. The paratroops were again spread out over a large area because of inaccurate drops, and many supplies were lost. Some of the paratroops eventually joined partisan groups in the area, while the main body restricted itself to night operations because of its lack of artillery and air support. A planned two- to three-day operation extended to almost five months, but despite incredible problems, the remnant of the 4th Airborne Corps managed to break through two encirclements (with the help of a battalion of reinforcements dropped into the area on 15—16 April) and to reach friendly lines by late May. Although it had created considerable havoc in the German rear, the corps was decimated. It had not accomplished its mission of preventing a German withdrawal to the west, because German counterblows had halted the main Russian advance.[17]

Despite the fact that not all Soviet night operations succeeded, the Germans came to perceive the Russian soldier as particularly well suited, both psychologically and physically, to fighting in the dark. Night has commonly been characterized as "no man's friend." Surrounded by darkness, people tend to imagine sinister forces lurking in quite harmless objects; every unknown sound seems ominous. Perceptions become distorted: objects appear larger than life, and distances appear greater and are more difficult to calculate. The psychological toll this can exact, when coupled with hunger, fatigue, and combat excitement, can engender near-panic or even mass hysteria among frontline troops.

Conditioned from childhood by frightening bedtime stories and by the comfort of artificial light, "civilized" people have a dread of night not shared by those who live "closer to nature."[18] Believing that the Russians lived "closer to nature" than themselves, the Germans conceded the ability of the Russian soldier, fighting in his own country, to orient and handle himself at night better than his German counterpart. They also respected the physical conditioning of the Russian soldier, his ability, for example, to lie in one position, on snow and ice in the bitter cold of a Russian winter, without movement for hours on end, patiently awaiting an opportunity to accomplish his mission.[19] (Such was the case in January 1942, when Soviet battalions persistently crossed over the frozen Sea of Azov by night, to spend all the next day lying motionless on the ice a few kilometers from the north bank. When night again fell, they raided the German billets and then retired as they had come. Heavy casualties due to exposure to the weather did not deter them.)

The battle of Stalingrad was a pivot point in the Russo-German conflict. On the night of 20 August 1942, even as the panzer and motorized infantry forces of the German 6th Army drove towards the Volga, elements of the Soviet 63d Army were crossing the Don River to the north. Forward detachments of about battalion strength, armed with automatic and antitank weapons, had started the initial crossing to the south bank at 0200. These detachments succeeded in surprising the defending outposts. First echelon battalions reinforced with the 45-mm and 76-mm regimental guns began crossing at 0300, although one battalion of the 197th Division was late and did not start crossing until 0500. German artillery temporarily halted, but did not stop, the determined Russian crossings, one of which was led by a battalion commander who dived into the river and swam to the far shore, followed by three hundred of his men. Despite problems generated by the swift current of the Volga, subunits of two adjacent Soviet divisions crossed to the south bank on ferries and rafts along a twenty-four-kilometer front. The main body of troops from the 197th Rifle Division and the 14th Guards Rifle Division overcame the defenders before the German reserves could reach the crossing sites or the Luftwaffe could be called upon. Second echelons crossed on 21 August, but German air harassment forced the main bodies, along with their artillery, to delay until night. By midnight the second echelons were across, and the 203d Rifle Division began its crossing, using improvised equipment and some ferries. The Soviets expanded the Don River bend bridgehead to 500 square kilometers and used it to launch the northern prong of the encirclement operation against the 6th Army of General Friedrich von Paulus. During the next three years, the Red Army would repeat this kind of night crossing many times on many rivers.[20]

The Soviets regard 19 November 1942 as the beginning of the second period of the war, during which the strategic balance shifted in their favor. The encirclement operation launched from the north by the 5th Tank Army on this date resulted in the seizure of the designated linkup point at Kalach, on the Don River, by forward detachments of the 26th Tank Corps on the night of 22 November. Russian tanks drove up with their headlights on, completely surprising the German defenders, who assumed they were friendly. When forces advancing from the south joined the 26th, the encirclement of the German 6th Army was complete.[21] In this offensive, the Russians pushed across the blizzardswept steppes by day and night, switching on their vehicle lights and following compass headings to landmarks. When enemy artillery fired upon them, they switched off the headlights, but the advance continued.[22]

In the weeks that followed, Russian armor stopped an attempt by the German 48th Panzer Corps to break the encirclement at Stalingrad. One of the key battles took place on the night of 25—26 December, when Soviet infantry supported by tanks captured the Shestakov bridge and occupied

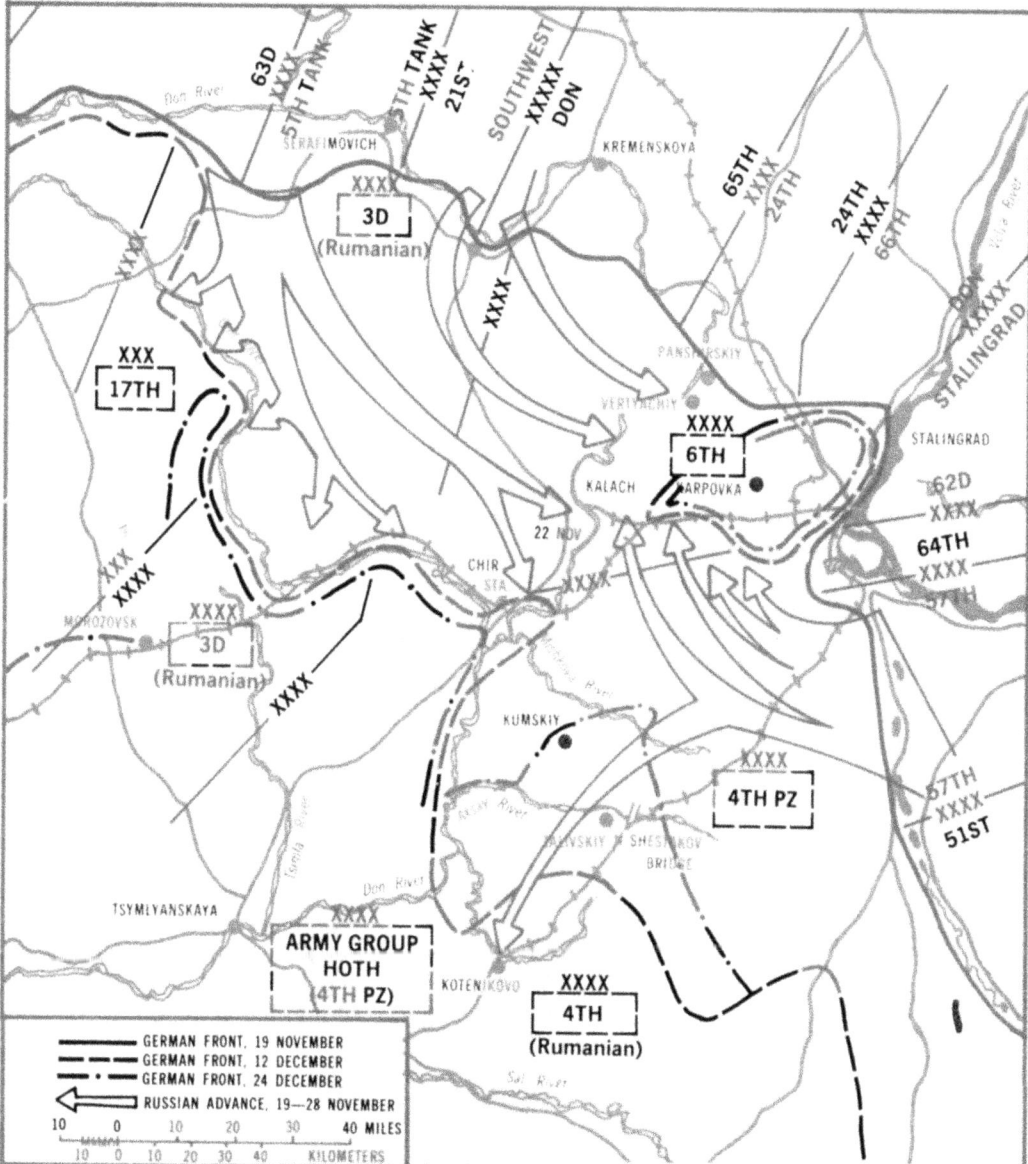

Map 2. Battle of Stalingrad

the town of Romashkin on the river Askay, fifty miles southwest of Stalingrad. Writing after the war, General Friedrich Wilhelm von Mellenthin, the chief of staff of the 48th Panzer Corps, described its destruction:

> The Russians did not stop their attacks when darkness fell, and they exploited every success immediately and without hesitation. Some of the Russian attacks were made by tanks moving in at top speed; indeed speed, momentum and concentration were the causes of their success. The main effort of the attacking Russian armor was speedily switched from one point to another as the situation demanded.[23]

By May 1943 the Soviets enjoyed an advantage over the Germans in both manpower and equipment. After the failure of the last great German offensive (Kursk, July 1943), the Russians began their planned summer offensive to take the Belgorod-Kharkov area, strike out for the Dnieper, and cross it in an effort to cut off the German withdrawal from the Donbas to the west. The Soviets, who had been experimenting with tank armies since Stalingrad, were now employing these new organizations as the mobile task force that would lead a front's offensive, after the front's assault group had created a gap to exploit success into the depth of enemy defenses, known as "operational depth."[24] In the tank battles for Kharkov, 17—20 August 1943, the Soviet 5th Guards Tank Army attempted to exploit the attack in operational depth for the Voronezh Front. Without effective air, artillery, or infantry support, however, it was unable to overcome the prepared defenses of 11th Infantry Corps and the 2d SS Panzer Division ("*Das Reich*") in daylight attacks. The Germans had effectively tied panther and

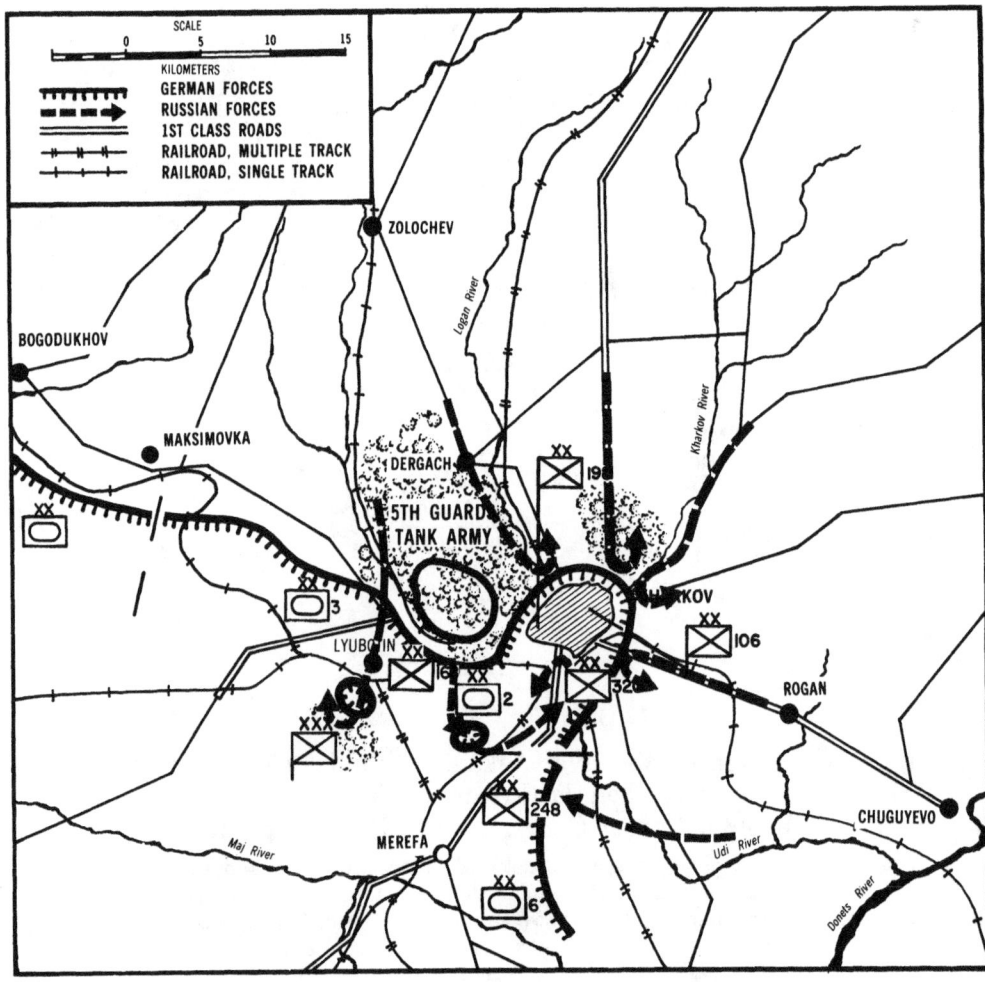

Map 3. Day and Night Attacks of the Soviet 5th Guards Tank Army at Kharkov

tiger tanks, self-propelled assault guns, 88-mm tank destroyers, and self-propelled 105-mm light field howitzers into their defense. Stuka dive bombers, using 1,800-kg heavy bombs intended originally for use against warships, took a heavy toll even before the battle began. The Soviets, therefore, resorted to night attacks on two successive nights. These desperate efforts were not entirely successful, but the Germans could claim only a Pyrrhic victory, for they soon had to abandon Kharkov because of their own heavy losses and Russian advances elsewhere on the front.[25]

By late September, the forces of four Soviet fronts were pursuing the retreating Germans back towards the 1,400-mile-long Dnieper River, a formidable obstacle the Germans called their East Wall. Unfortunately for the invaders, Hitler had prohibited fortification of the right bank of the Dnieper.[26] Under the pressure of time and in an effort to preclude a German buildup, the Soviet Army crossed the Dnieper along a 750-kilometer front in an operation that ran from 22 to 30 September 1943. Despite the fact that the Russians had no bridging capability (and would not until 1944), they were able to establish more than twenty bridgeheads on the right bank. Forward detachments marching at night forced most of these crossings. These detachments normally comprised a reinforced tank brigade with a self-propelled artillery regiment, and one or two battalions of artillery, with an engineer unit of up to battalion strength attached. They sometimes included infantry as well and generally operated forty or more kilometers in front of the tank or mechanized corps from which they came. They were usually sent out, without artillery preparation or air support, to seize bridgeheads, crossing on whatever boats or rafts they could gather or improvise from boards and dry logs.[27] If the opposite bank was fortified, they staged a false crossing elsewhere to divert German attention. Before morning, they concealed crossing materials and then withdrew or hid until they could continue the operation the next night. Some of the sites included bridges built below the water level to conceal them from the Luftwaffe. In one location, the Soviets puttied the openings on sixty tanks so that they could cross under water to the right bank.[28]

Russian bridgeheads, once established, became a source of great and immediate concern to the Germans. As General von Mellenthin explains:

> Bridgeheads in the hands of the Russians are grave danger indeed. It is quite wrong not to worry about bridgeheads, and to postpone their elimination. Russian bridgeheads, however small and harmless they may appear, are bound to grow into formidable danger-points in a very brief time and soon become insuperable strong points. A Russian bridgehead, occupied by a company in the evening, is sure to be occupied by at least a regiment the following morning and during the night will become a formidable fortress, well-equipped with heavy weapons and everything necessary to make it almost impregnable. No artillery fire, however violent and well concentrated, will wipe out a Russian bridgehead which has grown overnight. This Russian principle of 'bridgeheads everywhere' constitutes a most serious danger and cannot be overrated.[29]

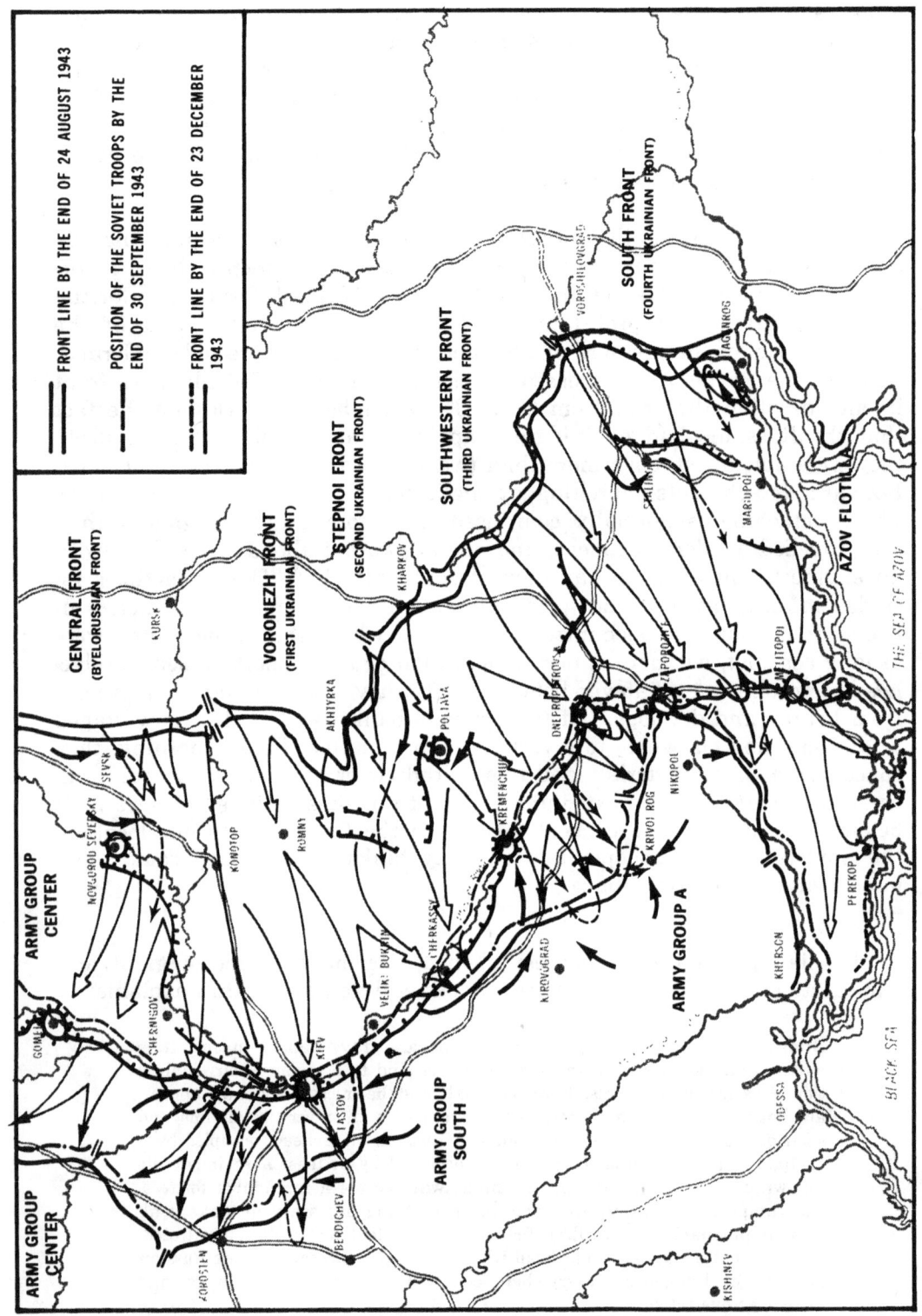

Map 4. Battle of the Dnieper/Airborne Insertion

Despite the problems encountered in the paratroop operation at Vyazma in 1942, the Soviets attempted a second night drop of an entire airborne corps on 24—25 September 1943 to seize a bridgehead at the Bukrin Bend on the Dnieper. Although the concept was excellent, the planning, timing, and execution of the operation produced results similar to those in 1942. The landing of the first two brigades, scheduled for the night of the twenty-third, had to be delayed a full day because of bad weather and the failure of all military transports to arrive at the three designated airfields. Although 4,575 paratroops were airborne the next night, a full 30 percent of the two brigades remained behind because of aircraft that never arrived, refueling problems, and the insistence of the pilots on carrying smaller lifts than the corps staff had planned. The pilots were inadequately trained, despite exercises held late that summer along the Moskva River, on terrain similar to the Dnieper. Nor were the pilots prepared for the strong antiaircraft resistance they encountered once the operation began. As a result, the two brigades (minus) were spread over a much wider zone than intended, landing between Rzishchev and Cherkassy. Some landed over friendly positions on the Russian-held side of the river; some landed in the river itself; worse, the main body landed on the positions of three German divisions moving through the area. The Germans shot at the parachutists while they were still in the air, thus forcing them to begin fighting before they hit the ground.[30]

Once on the ground, the paratroops (and what equipment they had not left behind) were so scattered that they were forced to operate in approximately thirty-five small groups. Their mission of seizing a bridgehead and holding a line 110 kilometers long and about twenty-six kilometers deep was no longer feasible, if indeed it ever had been. Instead, Soviet airborne troops once again assumed the role of guerrillas, hiding in forests by day and moving and fighting with partisan groups in the area by night. Because their radio gear was scattered over a wide area, they could not communicate with other Soviet forces. Plans to drop a third brigade were cancelled long before communications were reestablished on 6 October. Gradually, small groups of paratroops began to merge into a corps unit, and an estimated 1,000 or more finally linked up with the advancing forces of the Second Ukrainian Front in mid-November. The Soviets had gambled in conducting this operation at a time when bad weather precluded aerial reconnaissance of the target area. The result was a fiasco, which led Stalin to prohibit similar night operations.[31]

Hitler had ordered certain German bridgeheads on the Dnieper held at all costs. Among these were Zaporozh'e and Kiev, both of which figured prominently in the development of Soviet night operations. This was especially true of Zaporozh'e, which covered a forty-by-twenty-kilometer area, protected important iron and manganese ore regions in the Ukraine, contained a great hydroelectric dam and power station, and protected the flank of German forces in the Crimea. The battle for the bridgehead began on 1 October, pitting six and a half German divisions against three Soviet armies

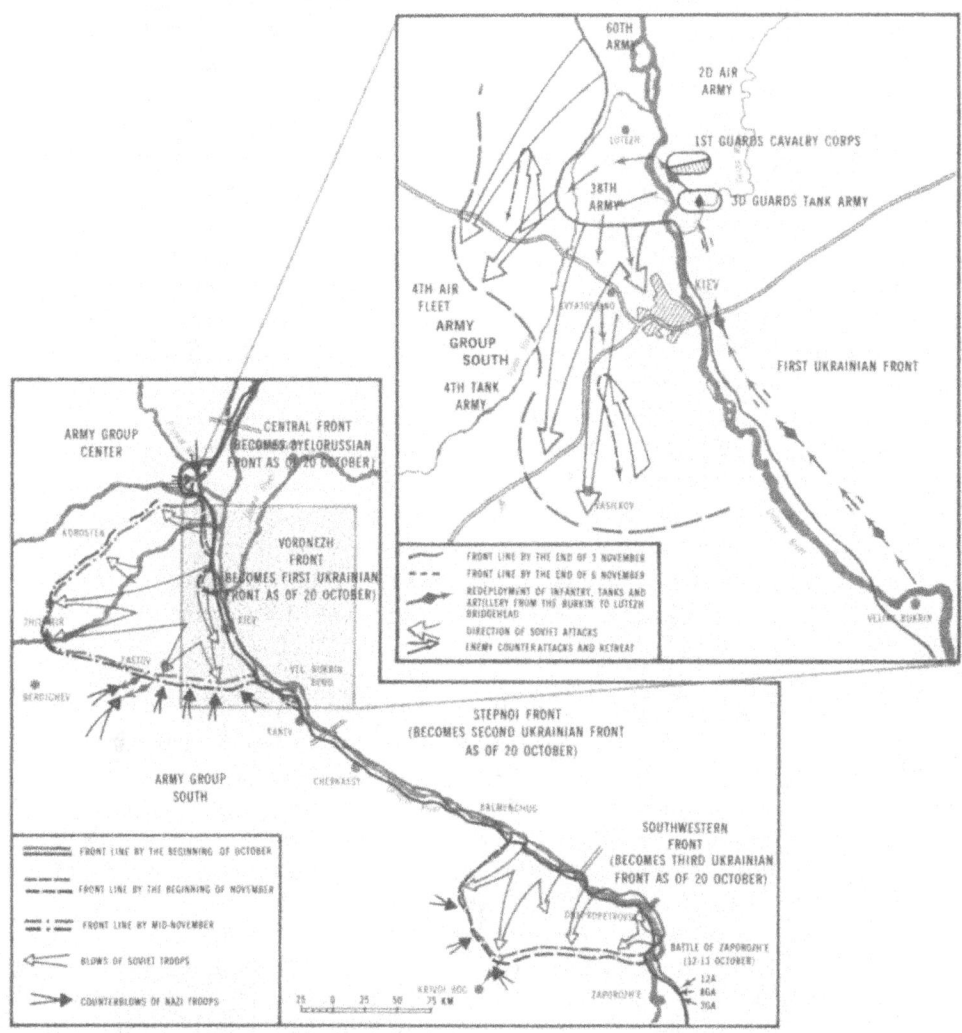

Map 5. Battles of Zaporozh'e and Kiev

approaching the west bank from the east (8th Guards Army), northeast (12th Army), and southeast (3d Guards Army). Although the Soviets, by this time, were receiving dedicated bomber support and had organized their artillery into independent divisions for more rapid concentration in a breakthrough, they were not at first able to penetrate the German defensive belts. The 8th Guards Army, according to Soviet accounts, had to repulse eleven counterattacks in one day. In the process, it began to use smoke screens to conceal tank destroyer assault teams. This method proved so successful that the Soviets organized three- to five-man teams under sergeants or officers to infiltrate the German defenses at night, to seek out panthers, tigers, and other powerful weapons. To counter this threat, the Germans began to withdraw their tanks from the first line of defense at night.

This weakening of the Germans' first line defense, along with the limited success achieved by the 12th Army on the night of 11 October, undoubtedly persuaded General V. I. Chuikov to launch a night attack with his own 8th Guards Army at 2310 on 12 October. After a massive ten-minute artillery preparation upon reconnoitered targets, Chuikov's tanks advanced five to six kilometers on his right flank, though units on the left advanced only one-half kilometer. General R. Malinovsky, the front commander, conferred with Chuikov on the results. He then ordered a concerted attack by all three armies for the night of 13 October and charged Chuikov with coordinating the actions of the tank and mechanized corps, which were to be committed simultaneously with the infantry on both flanks of the breakthrough. The two generals decided to rest a good portion of their forces for the night attack and to insure that the staffs concentrated on the night operation, rather than on the operation for the next day. At 2150 front artillery opened up a short, but massive preparation. The 8th Guards Army spearheaded the attack with reinforced rifle companies from three divisions, followed by main forces of infantry supported by tanks and artillery. Advancing at full speed, carrying assault troops, and employing flamethrowers, tanks overwhelmed the Germans' second defensive belt. The forces penetrated eight to ten kilometers, reached the suburbs of Zaporozh'e by morning, and fully occupied the city that day as the Germans withdrew.[32]

Chuikov and many of the men who fought in his army at Stalingrad were veterans of night combat in that beleaguered city. He personally advocated attacks under cover of darkness or smoke screens, noting that the "important thing is that . . . the commander should be sure to keep the directing of the battle in his grasp."[33] Thus, at Zaporozh'e, he determined the battle plan on a map and then made it more specific on the terrain. According to the plan, the infantry received substantial amounts of artillery (including 122-mm and 152-mm) for close support, with up to 30 percent of the guns used with direct laying. Officers riding in tanks equipped with radios adjusted artillery. Stakes with white arrows that were visible at night marked armor lines of advance. Tank companies received column guides chosen from infantry regimental officers, and two or three submachine gunners to designate targets and defend against tank destroyers. White geometrical figures painted on turrets, sides, and the rear areas of tanks provided easy identification. The plan also called for a company of engineers to breach minefields, antitank ditches, and other obstacles. Upon reaching designated lines during the advance, tank crews were to signal with headlights, infantry with flashlights. Planned illumination methods included flares for pointing out enemy positions or obstacles and paths around them, and a series of multicolored flares to mark the front line for supporting air. Tracers and shells designated targets. Because of this thorough preparation, the attack not only achieved surprise but also went considerably beyond a *limited* night operation and the guidance specified in the 1942 version of the Infantry Tactical Manual of the Red Army.[34]

Farther north along the Dnieper, Soviet arms again proved successful after overcoming initial obstacles. At Bukrin, the Second Ukrainian Front could not get its heavy artillery across the river without bridging equipment; nor could it break out of the bridgehead there in October. Consequently, it transferred its operation northward to the bridgehead at Lutezh. There, on 3 November, the 38th Army and the 3d Guards Tank Army broke out of the bridgehead. Continuing the advance on the evening of the fourth, the 38th Army made a penetration into which the tanks of the 3d Guards Tank Army moved. Despite the onset of darkness, the tanks, which had by this time jumped out in front of the infantry, continued to push forward, headlights on and sirens howling. The lights and sirens coupled with the massed firepower of the T-34 tanks exacted a heavy psychological toll upon many of the German defenders. Despite German counterattacks, the Soviets crossed the Irpen River five miles west of Kiev and continued their advance towards Fastov, an important communications center southwest of Kiev. Led by the 5th Guards Tank Corps, the Soviets stormed Kiev the night of 5—6 November 1943.[35]

The day-night attack of 4 November was the first time the Soviets had achieved surprise at night by having tanks attack with sirens blaring and headlights on. More important, it marked the beginning of an effort to employ second echelons effectively at night, thus maintaining around-the-clock pressure on the enemy. When the day portion of the battle had ended at Kiev, the Soviets maintained their momentum by continuing the attack at night and penetrating to a depth of seven to eight kilometers. Because this operation required careful coordination and planning, the Soviets spent half their time beforehand training at night, emphasizing such things as compass and terrain orientation. Divisional plans specified the forces and means of attack, the objectives, the departure zone at last light, the light signals for command and control, and the units designated to follow up the attack by daylight. Other areas of special interest were night reconnaissance, flank security, battle formations, ammunition supply (especially tracers), and illumination of the objective.[36]

The success of night operations in the second period of the war led to a greater use of this tactic in the third phase of the war, 1944—45 (one prominent Soviet expert has estimated that 40 percent of all Soviet attacks in 1944—45 were at night).[37] This increase was for the most part a by-product of the Soviet determination to maintain continuous pressure on the thinning and overextended German lines. The famous, but dwindling German mobile reserve could no longer effectively blunt rapid Soviet armor penetrations. A series of costly encirclements put the Germans in the uncomfortable position of having to attempt desperate night attacks to break out, much as the Soviets had had to do in 1941, when the situation was reversed.

Such was the case in the Korsun-Shevchenkovsky Operation, where the Soviets formed an inner ring around the remnants of eight German divisions and then set up an outer ring, seventy to eighty kilometers from the

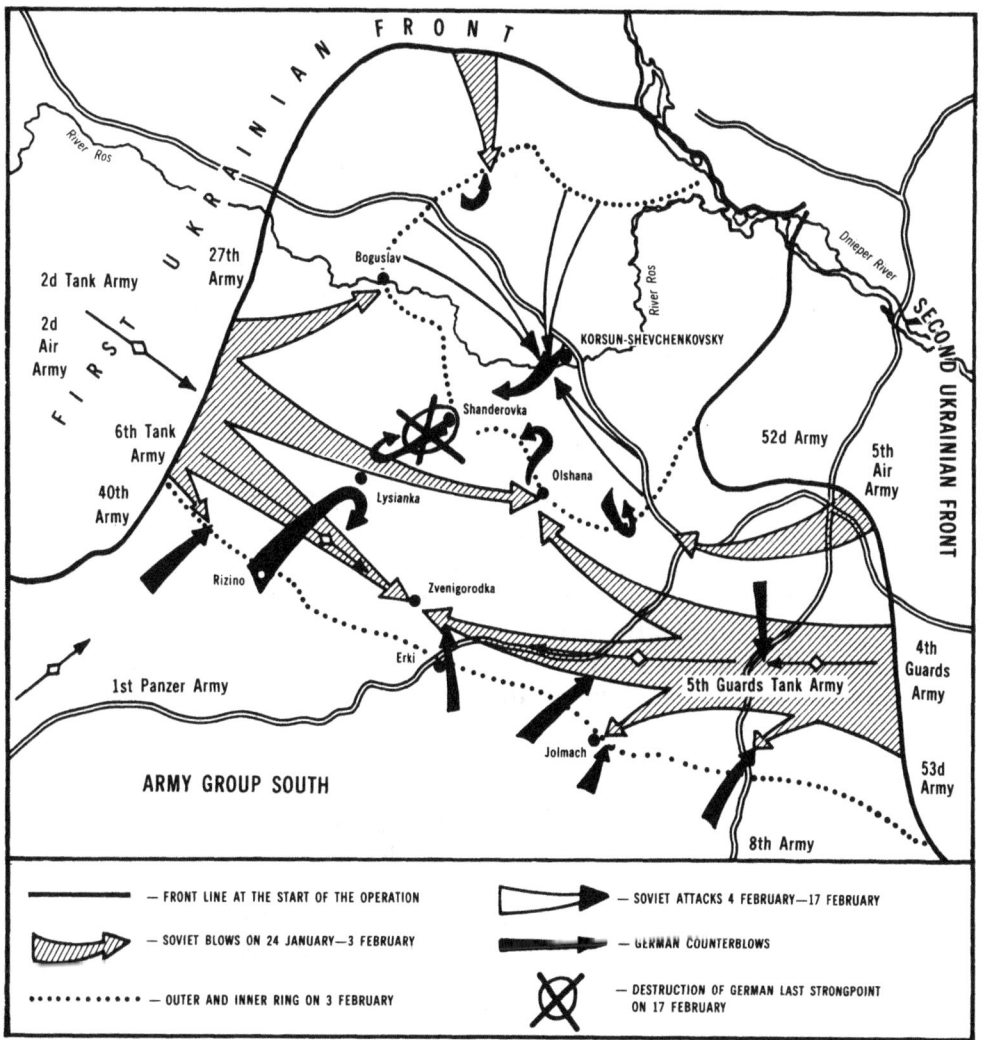

Map 6. Korsun-Shevchenkovsky Operation

first. Between the two rings, the Soviets concentrated artillery, which along with aviation, set about reducing the pocket piece by piece. After two weeks of encirclement, German forces outside the pocket could achieve only limited penetrations of the outer ring of Soviet armor. The Germans inside the pocket were therefore ordered to break out and they attempted to do so on the night of 16—17 February 1944,[38] a noteworthy night battle because of the Soviet bombing of the village of Shanderovka. Although night bomber aviation had accompanied the 4th Mechanized Corps in the Mius Operation in August 1943, night bomber support was the exception rather than the rule. But on the night of 16—17 February, Soviet aviation dared to attempt night bombing, primarily at the behest of General I. Konev, the front commander, who was determined to deny the Germans in the pocket any respite. On this dark, blizzardswept night, slow U-2 aircraft used incendiaries to burn Shanderovka and to light up the target. The extent of the disaster the Germans suffered during their subsequent attempt to break the encirclement southwest of Shanderovka at the nearby village of Lysianka remains in dispute.[39]

The Soviets continued to press the Germans during the spring thaw period (March-April), when muddy roads normally halted all offensive operations. The Soviets concentrated their efforts, including night operations, in the extreme south, the only part of the Ukraine that remained in German hands. In the Bereznegovatoye-Snigirevka Operation, for example, the Third Ukrainian Front employed a cavalry mechanized group to pursue withdrawing forces on the night of 6 March 1944. This move was unusual in that the front's mobile group, consisting of cavalry and mechanized forces, was not as mobile as the armor and hence was not usually employed where it might interfere with armored operations. In this situation, however, pouring rain and muddy roads favored the use of the cavalry mechanized group, which was sent into a gap at 2200 and advanced eleven kilometers, thus facilitating the next day's offensive. Three weeks later, on 27 March, the front employed a night attack to break through the main line of defenses in the Odessa Operation. In this case, the Soviets attacked at night because they lacked sufficient numbers of direct-support tanks and were dissatisfied with their artillery densities.[40] Nevertheless, they took Odessa by 10 April.

The successful advance of the Fourth Ukrainian Front, farther south on the Kerch peninsula, forced the Germans and Rumanians to begin a withdrawal there as well. This time the Soviets enjoyed overwhelming superiority in all areas, but again chose a night attack, conducted by General Yeremenko's Special Black Sea Army (the 51st Separate Coastal Army), to launch their offensive. On the night of 10—11 April reconnaissance battalions initiated the pursuit, followed by division advanced battalions and mobile groups of the corps. By 1100 the next day, the unexpected night attackers had advanced seventy kilometers.[41]

On the third anniversary of the German invasion of Russia, 22 June 1944, the Soviets initiated a massive offensive against Army Group Center in Byelorussia, the last deep German salient remaining on Russian territory. The Germans, anticipating that the Soviets would continue to follow up on their success in the south, were not prepared to cope with the forces of four Soviet fronts approaching from diverging directions to cut off German strongholds at Vitebsk, Orsha, Mogilev, Bobruisk, and Minsk. The result was a succession of swift encirclements by superior Soviet forces. In the Vitebsk section, Soviet forces kept their buildup secret by regrouping units under cover of night. Soviet troops continued to dig defensive positions despite their offensive intentions. Vastly superior numbers of Russian aircraft also hindered German reconnaissance. On a frontage of five hundred kilometers, eleven armies, each preceded by reinforced advanced battalions

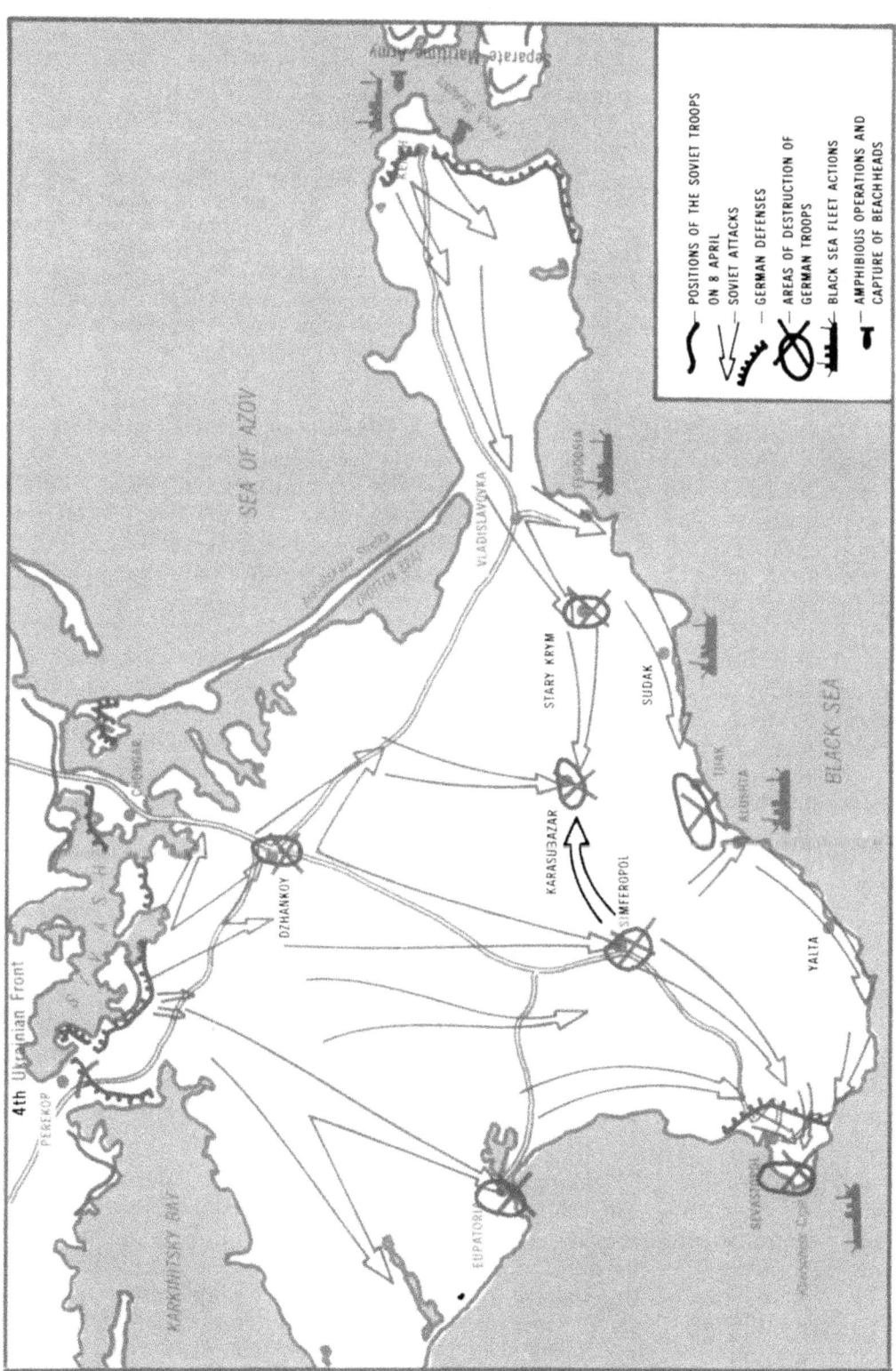

Map 7. Crimean Offensive

conducting reconnaissance in force, initiated the offensive in the Byelorussian campaign.[42] In one portion of the Vitebsk sector, the reconnaissance conducted the morning before the general offensive proved unsuccessful. The Soviets therefore launched a night attack, with each participating battalion supported by fifty to sixty artillery pieces. According to General Kuznetsov:

> The attack started at 4:00 A.M. In view of the fact that our units and the troops of the enemy were in direct contact, the artillery opened fire simultaneously with the beginning of the advance. The weapons of direct laying conducted fire against previously reconnoitered fire positions, and the rest of the artillery neutralized areas in which one supposed there were mortars and artillery positions. The attack was successfully executed: of all the battalions participating in it only one failed to break into the enemy dispositions; the rest captured one or two trenches of the enemy and made it possible for our troops to undertake an all-out offensive at daybreak....[43]

Using a pincer movement, the forces of two Soviet fronts soon cut off Vitebsk. While operations continued to move westward, elements of the 39th Army infiltrated into the center of the city on the night of 25—26 June, capturing the only bridge in the city left standing over the Western Dvina. Joined by elements of the 43d Army, they cleared the city of the German occupation force by morning. This encirclement battle alone cost the Germans 20,000 killed and 10,000 captured.[44]

To the south, the forces of the First Byelorussian Front completed the encirclement of Bobruisk on 27 June. Bombing and strafing by five hundred attack planes, followed by a ground attack of infantry and armor, frustrated German efforts to break out that night. Two German efforts the next night not only failed, but also gave the Soviets the opportunity to cross the Berezina River east of Bobruisk and enter the city at 0400. Attacks from the south and west completed the investment and capture of Bobruisk and resulted in heavy tolls of Germans killed and captured.[45]

In the desperate fighting in Byelorussia, the Germans managed to surround a division of the 43d Army. Not even a Russian tank corps could break through the German antitank defenses. General A. P. Beloborodov, the commander of the 43d Army, therefore sought the permission of the new front commander, General I. K. Bagramyan, and the *Stavka* representative, General A. M. Vasilevsky, to conduct a mass tank attack at night with headlights on. The attack resulted in the destruction of eighty German tanks and the capture of sixty guns and twelve hundred prisoners.[46]

The campaign in Byelorussia resulted in the complete destruction of Army Group Center, including at least twenty-five divisions and 350,000 men. Among the offensives that followed was the Lublin-Brest Operation, an example of the day-night operations conducted by General Chuikov's 8th Guards Army, in this case directed against Army Group North Ukraine. Operating thirty kilometers west of Kovel on 18 July 1944, the 88th, among other divisions, penetrated the first line of German defenses. Following a

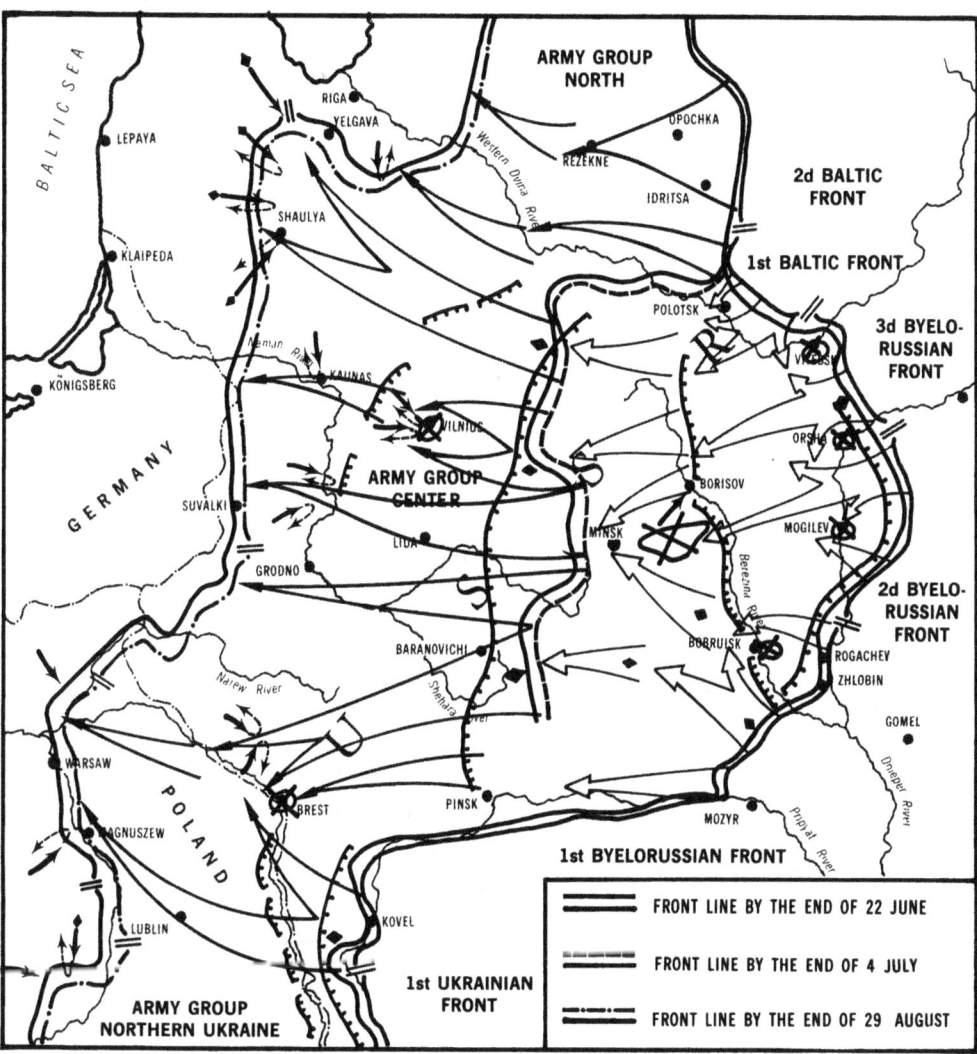

Map 8. Byelorussian Campaign

ten-minute artillery preparation, the 88th Division advanced four more kilometers that night by committing its regimental second echelons (consisting of a reinforced infantry battalion from each regiment). Main forces from the division continued the attack the next day until the Germans halted them about 1700 along an intermediate defensive line. That night on Chuikov's order the 88th Division, assisted by the second echelon 39th Guards Rifle Division (from the 28th Guards Infantry Corps), fought its way towards objectives on the Western Bug. Commencing at 2000, after a fifteen-minute artillery preparation, the attacking units reached a depth of five kilometers by 0530. On 20 July, the 8th Guards Army forced the river, pursuing the withdrawing Germans almost to Chelm on the road to Lublin.[47]

In the Vistula-Oder and East Prussian offensives of 1945, the Soviets again achieved high tempos of operation by the introduction of second echelon regiments and divisions at night and by the use of reinforced forward or advanced detachments in nighttime pursuit. By this time, Soviet night operations were coming of age. The Soviets were training specific units for specific roles.[48] To prepare for the offensive in East Prussia (13 January—25 April), each infantry division had three battalions trained for assault of a fortified zone, two battalions for pursuit operations, three battalions for night operations, and one for the role of "leading mobile detachment." Up to one-half of the training was at night, and second echelons of some rifle divisions, such as the 5th Guards Rifle Corps of the 39th Army, switched to a nighttime regimen.[49] On successive nights in mid-January, specially trained battalions from the second echelons of the 17th and 19th Guards Rifle Divisions of this corps facilitated exploitation by main forces during the day.

Pursuit operations at night also employed reinforced infantry battalions serving as advanced detachments. On the night of 16 January, for example, advanced detachments from the 65th Army overcame German resistance and pushed forward in separate directions to depths of six to ten kilometers. Special plans were developed for reconnaissance, flank security (always a Soviet concern), and resupply.[50]

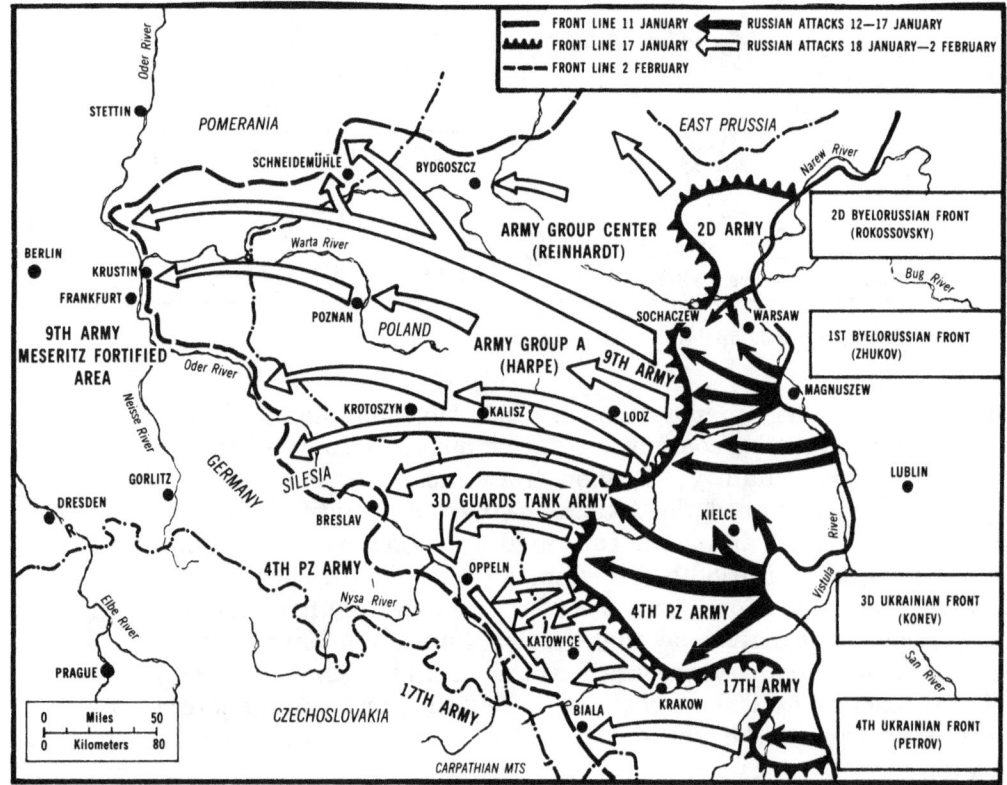

Map 9. Advance to the Oder

The Soviets also used forward detachments for pursuit operations in the Vistula-Oder campaign (12 January—7 February). One pertinent example, which occurred on the night of 16 January, was the capture of the town of Grojec by a forward detachment of the 9th Guards Tank Corps. By 2300 the Soviets had also initiated an attack on Sochaczew, thus cutting off German withdrawal to the west of Warsaw.[51] Operating primarily at night, this detachment later advanced ninety kilometers. A second example occurred on the night of 29—30 January, when the 44th Brigade, a forward detachment of the 11th Guards Tank Corps, succeeded in breaching the Meseritz fortified area, between Poznan and Kustrin. This operation was significant because it was undertaken on the initiative of the brigade commander, who was functioning as the vanguard of the 1st Tank Army. The army commander described Meseritz as

> ...a city of ferro-concrete and steel with underground railways, factories and electric power stations. It could hold a whole army. Armored shafts went underground to a depth of 30—40 meters. On the surface the approaches were blocked with anti-tank obstacles covering many kilometers. Dozens of low domes of the permanent weapons emplacements were studded with gun and machine-gun barrels. The nearby lakes were connected with a system of dams, which in case of need, could flood any sections of the fortified area.[52]

Taking advantage of the darkness and the limited number of German sentries on duty, Colonel Gusakovsky, a commander known for his daring, directed combat engineers to remove railway spikes blocking the road. Then, standing on the road, facing away from the defenders, these engineer troops used flashlights on their belts to guide Soviet tanks into action. Although the Germans opened irregular artillery and mortar fire at the sound of the tank engines, they were too late. The Soviet tank crews returned the fire and pressed on, clearing the area by 0300. The brigade thus slipped through a supposedly "impenetrable area" without losing a tank and was able to conduct a successful ambush the next morning before linking up with Soviet forces bypassing the once again "impenetrable" Meseritz fortified area. The successful Vistula-Oder Operation brought the Soviets and their Polish allies 310 miles in twenty-three days, an average advance of twelve to fourteen miles a day, though not without serious losses to their forces.[53]

In many ways the battle of Berlin was the culmination of the growth process for Soviet night operations, although as we shall see, their maturity was to be evidenced on a grander scale in Manchuria later that summer. Soviet commanders made extensive efforts to prepare for the Berlin Operation. Although the Soviets might have attacked the city as early as February 1945, Marshal Georgii Zhukov thought the risks too great and instead deliberately halted the First Byelorussian Front in order to resupply his armies and to make every possible preparation for an overwhelming and successful assault.[54] Zhukov had boldly planned a front-wide night attack

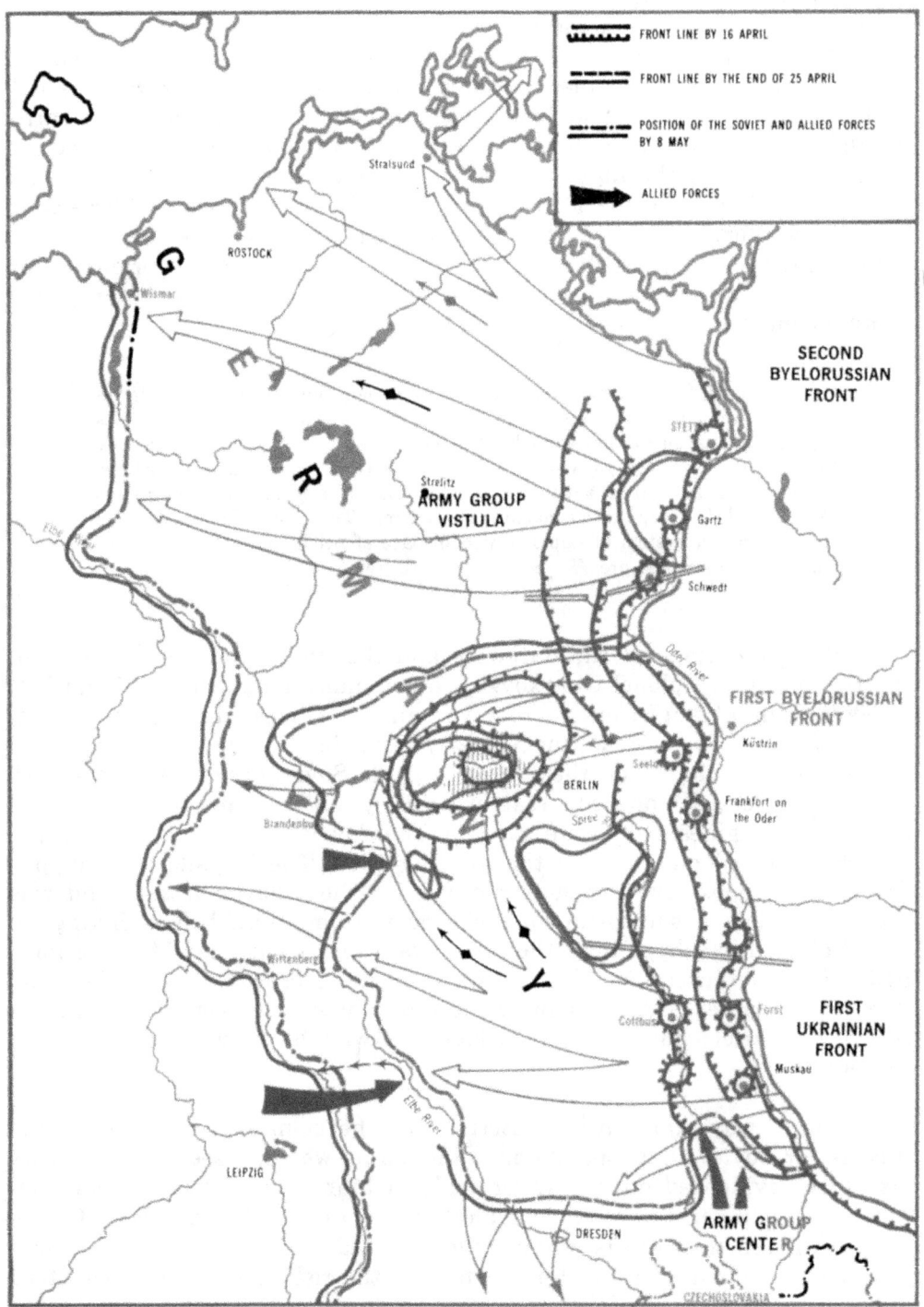

Map 10. The Battle of Berlin

for the First Byelorussian Front, employing 140 searchlights to illuminate the German defenses.[55] Before launching the attack, the Soviets undertook extensive reconnaissance of enemy dispositions and artillery and carefully studied maps and relief sketches.[56] Troops, down to company level, received detailed sketches of enemy defenses based on photographs. The Soviets trained column leaders, designated from among noncommissioned and commissioned officers in each company and battalion, to orient themselves in the area at night, to use a compass, and to employ various means of signal communication with adjacent units. Plans also included special guides, designated for each tank and self-propelled gun, and aviation support to bomb artillery positions and important deep objectives.[57]

The breakout of the First Byelorussian Front from the Kustrin bridgehead, only sixty-four kilometers from Berlin, was to initiate the battle, while the First Ukrainian Front of Marshal Konev, farther to the south on the Neisse, was to destroy the forces of Army Group Center south of the German capital. Konev, however, was ordered to be ready to attack Berlin from the south in the event Zhukov's front was held up on the eastern approaches to the city. Unlike Zhukov, his peer and competitor, Konev did not intend to use searchlights, because he wanted to cross the Neisse under cover of complete darkness. Instead, he ordered two hours and twenty-five minutes of artillery preparation to cover the entire crossing operation and employed Soviet aircraft along a 390-kilometer front to create extensive smoke screens to hinder enemy observation when darkness lifted.[58]

What one historian has called the "most elaborate offensive ever mounted by the Red Army"[59] began with an earsplitting and awesome artillery preparation best described by Zhukov himself:

> We concentrated a huge striking force on the bank of the Oder: the supply of shells alone enough for a million artillery rounds on the first day of the storming. To stun the German defenses immediately, it was decided to begin storming at night with the use of powerful searchlights. Finally the famous night of April 16 began. No one could sleep. Three minutes before zero hour we left our dugout and took up places at our observation posts. To my dying day I will remember the land along the Oder, blanketed in April fog. At 5:00 A.M. [0300 Berlin time] sharp it all began. The Katyushas struck, over 20,000 guns opened fire, hundreds of bomber planes roared overhead... and after 30 minutes of fierce bombing and shelling, 140 anti-aircraft searchlights employed every 650 feet in a line, were turned on. A sea of light swept over the enemy, blinding them, and pointing out in the darkness the objects of attack for our tanks and infantry.[60]

Army Group Vistula, commanded by General Gotthard Heinrici, had withdrawn from its first line of defenses earlier that night in anticipation of the rockets and artillery. Hence the Russians met comparatively little resistance in the first hour and a half of the attack. The troops began moving forward at 0320 behind a double moving barrage of artillery (for the first two kilometers), followed by a single barrage (for two more kilometers). The bright searchlights and the artillery fire broke the darkness of night. Although the use of searchlights had worked well in the war games conducted before the battle, General Chuikov, writing years after the war, felt that early historians of the war were wrong in their judgments of its success. He noted that periodically turning the searchlights on and off (probably to prevent them from becoming too lucrative a target) momentarily blinded and disoriented the Soviets' own troops. He also pointed out that battlefield haze from the powder, smoke, and dust (not to mention the fog noted by Zhukov) limited the effective range of searchlights to 150—200 meters. In any case, vehicles and troops in many areas halted in front of the many streams and canals of the Oder Valley, as battlefield coordination between artillery, infantry, and tanks broke down. Chuikov also suffered a rebuke from the hard-driving Zhukov when it became known about noon that his (Chuikov's) soldiers were pinned down in front of the well-defended Seelow Heights. Zhukov then immediately ordered in the 1st Guards Tank Army over Chuikov's protest. This jammed the already crowded roads upon which the Soviets depended (cross-country movement over the surrounding heavily mined and marshy terrain was impractical). On the first night of the operation, the Soviets had advanced almost four kilometers before German resistance stopped them. Although Russian units had breached the second line of German defenses in some areas before noon, the First Byelorussian Front as a whole continued to meet considerable opposition and made only slow progress.[61]

To the south, Konev's forces advanced up to thirteen kilometers the first day, thanks in part to the use of smoke. Unbeknownst to Zhukov, on 17 April Stalin phoned Konev to approve the latter's plan to turn his tank armies toward Berlin. The 3d Guards Tank Army forced the Spree on the night of 17—18 April and broke into Berlin from the south on the night of 20—21 April. The next day elements of three armies from Zhukov's command reached the outskirts of the city. Fierce street to street and house by house combat began in the city on 21 April. After the completion of the city's encirclement in the west on the twenty-fifth, its reduction by successive deep thrusts towards its center was only a matter of time. Zhukov had ordered a small scale model of the city made for his staff and had carefully schooled his troops in street fighting. Commanders like Chuikov had considerable experience in this brand of warfare, dating back to Stalingrad and, more recently, to Poznan.[62] In spite of their advantages in terms of numbers of fighting men, artillery, tanks, and self-propelled weapons, the Soviets selected night attacks for taking important city objectives, major strongpoints, or objectives that required crossing canals. As usual, Soviet procedures were methodical, including reconnaissance before every engagement. General Kuznetsov, the commander of the 3d Shock Army, observed that the greatest successes at night came from platoon- to company-size units. Bombing and artillery strikes preceded every assault, and guards mortars, self-propelled mounts, flamethrowers, demolitions, and artillery batteries with heavy guns reinforced the infantry. After bitter fighting, the resistance ended on 2 May 1945.[63]

The Soviet onslaught on Berlin was eminently successful, despite very high casualties on both sides (to be expected in urban warfare in a city the size of the German capital). The battle, however, was disappointing in some respects from a tactical standpoint because the considerable buildup for the operation was not carried out secretly, as prescribed by the 1944 Field Service Regulations and as had been the case in past operations, where this extra effort paid great dividends.[64] Also, the Soviet reconnaissance in strength, consisting of thirty-two battalions sent out two days before the attack at 0740 on 14 April was not used to develop the offensive or to upset German expectations of when the main blow would strike. These instances called for night operations, but, for whatever reasons, the Soviets did not use them. The Soviets would not, however, repeat these mistakes in the Manchurian campaign, which followed on the heels of the struggle in Europe.[65]

Historians have acknowledged the speed and shock effect of the German blitzkrieg that rolled over Europe in the early stages of the war, but have said little about what the Soviets accurately describe as their lightning warfare of August 1945 in Manchuria. Soviet rates of advance during the final stages of the war in Europe had equaled those of the Germans in Russia in 1941, thanks in part to the Russians' emphasis on day-night operations and night attacks.[66] During the course of years of constant fighting, Soviet night operations had evolved from silent small unit attacks with cold steel to complicated combined arms operations at the front level, as in the Berlin Operation, supported by air armies of night bombers. The campaign against the Japanese in Manchuria epitomized what the Soviets had learned by fighting the Germans. The degree of strategic surprise achieved in the Far East surpassed that achieved by the Germans in Operation Barbarossa. The time-sensitive nature of the Manchurian campaign, the great distances covered, and the swiftness and totality of victory led one Soviet general and historian to characterize this campaign as "the shortest campaign of World War II with the highest outcomes."[67] As might be expected by the results, night operations played a significant role.

Soviet operations in the Manchurian campaign followed by three months the end of the war in Europe on 8 May 1945. So long as the Soviet heartland was threatened by Hitler's armies, Stalin refused to declare war on Japan. Nevertheless, the Soviets felt compelled to maintain a force of thirty-five to forty divisions on the Manchurian border, despite the Soviet-Japanese Neutrality Pact of April 1941. At the Yalta Conference in early 1945, Stalin promised that once the war with Germany was over, the Soviet Union would assist its allies in the war against Japan. In keeping with this pledge, the Soviets, in April 1945, began serious preparations for a campaign in the Far East. They spared no effort in their transfer of men and materiel to the new front. They shipped the equivalent of more than thirty divisions and tremendous amounts of war materiel 9,000 to 12,000 kilometers, from eastern Europe via the Trans-Siberian Railway to the three front-level commands being established respectively on the northwest (the

Trans-Baikal Front), northeast (the Second Far Eastern Front), and eastern (the First Far Eastern Front) borders of Manchuria. Each of these fronts received commanders, staffs, and units who could be expected to perform missions and operate upon terrain similar to what they had experienced in Europe. Thus, the 6th Guards Tank and 53d Armies went to the Trans-Baikal Front because their experience in the Carpathian mountains, it was believed, would better enable them to meet the challenges of crossing the Greater Khingan mountains of western Manchuria. The 39th and 5th Armies went from East Prussia to the Trans-Baikal and First Far Eastern Fronts, respectively, because of their experience in crossing fortified zones similar to ones the Japanese had constructed in Manchuria. The Soviets also created a theater-level command under Marshal Vasilevsky to face the challenge of the enormous spaces and extremely rugged mountain-desert-taiga terrain of Manchuria. By August the three fronts contained an aggregate of 1,500,000 men, 26,000 guns and mortars, 5,500 tanks and self-propelled guns, and 3,800 aircraft.[68]

Although the Japanese occupied good defensive terrain and a series of strongly fortified zones, the Kwantung Army was a shell of its former self. Most of its reliable forces had gone to other theaters. Only six of its divisions had existed before January 1945. Its strength, even when including forces in Korea, southern Sakhalin, and the Kuriles, numbered only about 1.2 million men. Of greater significance, Japanese forces in Manchuria proper had only 1,155 tanks, or just over one-fifth as many as the Soviets. Furthermore, Soviet tanks had more armor and outgunned those of the Japanese. The Soviets enjoyed a similar advantage in artillery pieces and had twice as many aircraft. Although the Japanese failed to assess the Soviet threat properly or to detect the extent of the Soviet force buildup, they did recognize their own lack of combat readiness. When the attack came, they were in the process of a strategic reorientation, shifting from an offensive strategy to one of delaying at the borders, then employing stronger defensive lines once the enemy penetrated deeper into Manchuria. The idea, of course, was to mount a successively stronger resistance as the enemy exhausted his manpower and overextended his logistical lifeline.[69]

In contrast to the Berlin Operation, the Soviets, for their part, took greater precautions to achieve surprise, including conducting in secrecy all troop movements from west to east (including two front commands, three field armies, and one tank army). Only four men knew all the plans in each front or army. Written decisions appeared only on maps, and all orders were oral. The Soviets maintained a normal routine on the frontier, did not move the civilian population, and did not cancel leaves for troops on Sakhalin island until hostilities broke out. Troops concentrated only at night. The Trans-Baikal Front stored all equipment in camouflage shelters and used PO—2 observation planes to verify the effectiveness of this effort. Radio traffic patterns remained normal. In the area of the First Far Eastern Front, from Khabarovsk to the Lake Khanka region, arriving 5th Army troops detrained only at night and did not stay in population centers. Work

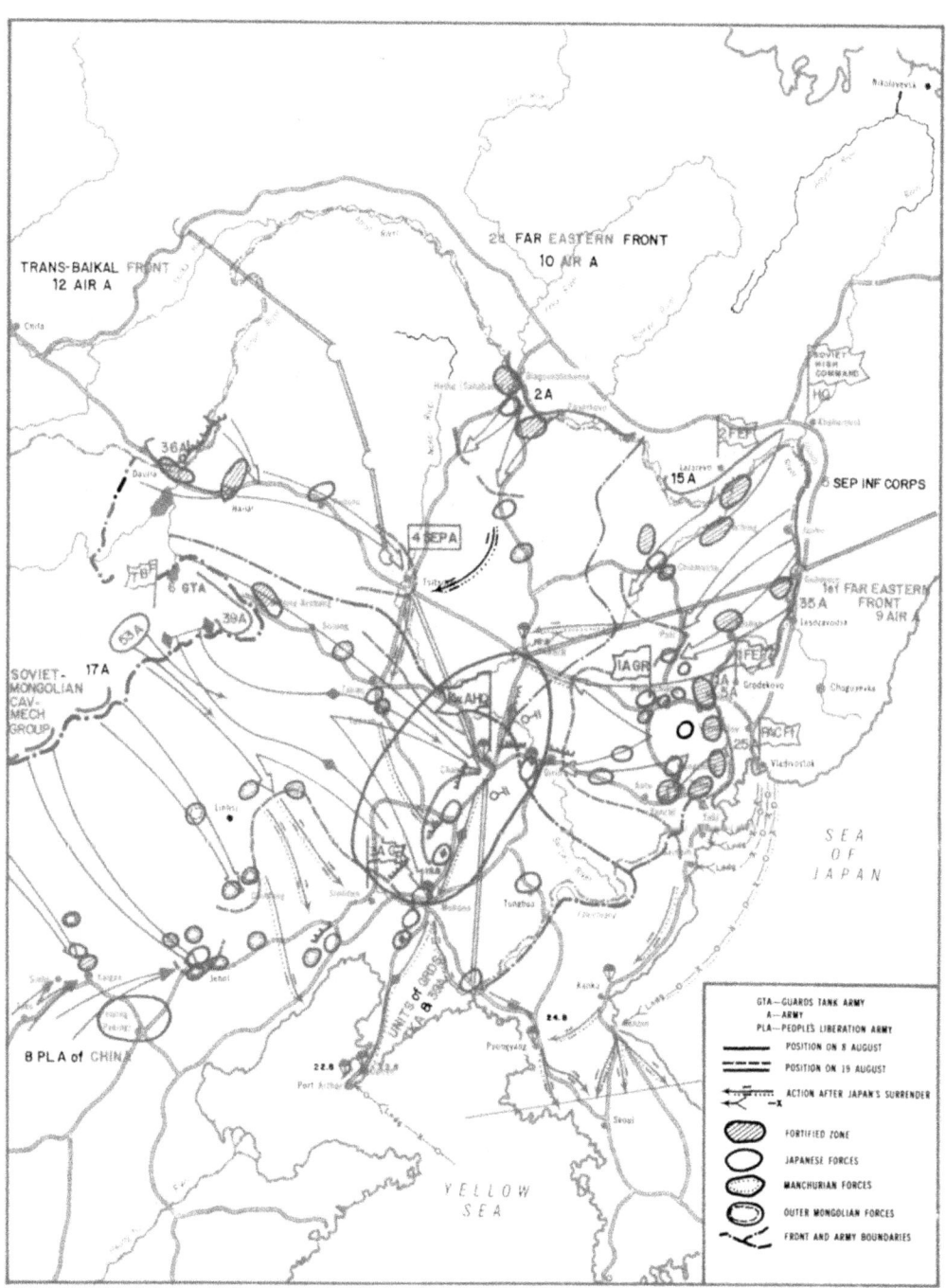

Map 11. The Manchurian Campaign

on defensive fortifications continued on this front, and a dummy concentration was formed in a secondary direction. Soviet commanders came to the Far East in disguise. (Marshal Meretskov, First Far Eastern Front commander, rode across the taiga in the uniform of a border guard in order to make a personal reconnaissance.) Finally, the Russians attacked in the rainy season, just as they had against the Germans in the spring of 1944. All in all, the Red Army sought and attained a high measure of strategic surprise in its Manchurian venture.[70]

An essential feature of the surprise effort called for almost simultaneous night attacks by all three fronts shortly after midnight on 9 August. Units were to cross the frontier after marching twenty to eighty kilometers from assembly areas located in the rear. Armor-heavy forces operating on separate, multiple axes were to thrust into the heart of Manchuria after penetrating the border defenses, which were formidable only in the sector of the First Far Eastern Front. The forces of the Trans-Baikal and First Far Eastern Fronts were to link up in south central Manchuria, thus dividing and enveloping Japanese forces before they had time to withdraw and create strong interior defensive lines. The main attack was to be that of the Trans-Baikal Front, whose advanced detachments began the offensive at 0010 and were followed by the main forces at 0430. Because the emphasis was on speed and preempting Japanese defenses, the Soviets employed strong forward detachments to initiate the attack on this front and to lead the attack after the initial breakthrough by assault units on the other two fronts, thus creating momentum for main forces. These detachments consisted primarily of armor and mechanized forces reinforced with self-propelled artillery and engineer units individually tailored to the terrain and situation they expected to encounter.

The scarcity of Japanese defenses and the need for speed, strength, and surprise resulted in the decision to have the 6th Guards Tank Army function, in effect, as the forward detachment for the Trans-Baikal Front. Because the Japanese had acted upon the assumption that the 2,000-meter peaks of the 300-kilometer-wide Grand Khingan mountain chain would preclude a major attack from this direction, Soviet artillery and air preparations were unnecessary. Traveling over the semidesert mostly by night in order to spare the tank engines and the men, the tanks of the 6th Guards Tank Army had raced 150 kilometers to the approaches of the mountain passes by nightfall on the ninth. To the south, almost unopposed, the 17th Army and the Soviet-Mongolian Cavalry Mechanized Group pushed east some fifty to fifty-five kilometers on separate, multiple axes. To the north of the 6th Guards Tank Army's spearhead, the 39th and 36th Armies advanced almost sixty kilometers on widely separated, but somewhat parallel axes.[71]

Only the 36th Army, operating on the front's northern flank and advancing on two axes, met any substantial resistance. On the tenth, an army forward detachment, reinforced by a tank destroyer battalion, a rocket launcher regiment, a light artillery regiment, a self-propelled artillery battalion, and a small-caliber antiaircraft regiment, crossed the rainswollen Argun River. Its commander, General V. A. Burmasov, decided to make a preemptive night attack on Hailar. To this end, he employed a bold, but difficult to control pincer movement by two forces. The 205th Tank Brigade conducted a turning movement to attack from the northeast, capturing a rail yard and a worker community on the outskirts of the city by 2300 before being halted. Its companion unit, the 152d Rifle Regiment, also traveling east of the city to bypass its fortifications, made a long swing south on motor vehicles to attack from the southeast. By morning determined resistance had held it up on the fringes of the city. This delay, which lasted six hours, disrupted the timetable for what had been planned as a simultaneous attack with the 205th. As a result, the two-pronged assault was only partially successful. The 205th Tank Brigade was pulled out of the city to continue the advance towards the Greater Khingan passes. The city fell to the Soviets after two days of unopposed air strikes and attacks by the 94th Rifle Division (which had replaced the 205th Tank Brigade) and the 293d Rifle Division. The fortified area northwest and southwest of the city held out until 18 August, when artillery and air strikes completed its reduction.[72]

On 9 August, the First Far Eastern Front, moving from the Primorye coastal region in the east, with three combined armies and a mechanized corps, struck the Japanese First Area Army in the most heavily fortified of the border areas. A torrential rainstorm forced the front to postpone its night attack scheduled for one minute after midnight. Frontier guards, who were familiar with many of the Japanese fortifications, nonetheless conducted a reconnaissance in force thirty minutes before the movement of the assault units at 0100. Company commanders carried detailed maps of Japanese defenses based on intelligence collected from radio intercepts, ground observation reports, and the limited aerial reconnaissance possible before the declaration of war. Heavy rain and fog caused the Soviets to cancel both the front-wide artillery preparation and the intended use of searchlights to blind and stun Japanese defenders. Nonetheless, the attack in such horrendous weather caught the Japanese completely by surprise. Strongpoint garrisons awoke to find themselves already bypassed by some Soviet units and under attack by others.[73]

The fortified border zone was forty kilometers long and thirty kilometers deep and contained 295 permanent emplacements, more than 100 of which had reinforced concrete shelters and armored cupolas. One of the most formidable of these was the iron bastion on Camel Hill, a double-humped mountain surrounded by three rivers and swampy terrain. Camel's fortifications included rings of escarpments, deep antitank ditches, and barbed wire entanglements six rows deep, as well as permanent emplacements with 305-mm and 410-mm gun mounts. During the night, the Soviets emplaced and camouflaged self-propelled guns and field guns to spearhead and support the attack on Camel at daybreak. A battalion of the 144th Rifle Division circled the hill under cover of darkness in preparation for the assault. The success at Camel and the methods used to achieve it were not unique. The Soviets overcame or bypassed all other frontier fortresses on the first day of the offensive, and Soviet artillery and aviation subsequently reduced them. Having achieved tactical surprise, the rifle divisions of the 5th Army had advanced four to six kilometers on the night of 9 August.[74]

As in the Trans-Baikal sector, armies of the First Far Eastern Front in eastern Manchuria attacked on separate axes in multiple columns. Command and control therefore presented a tremendous challenge, particularly at night. Unlike the Trans-Baikal Front, the forces of the First Far Eastern Front operated in a single echelon, which facilitated a speedier passage over the difficult, poorly mapped, and almost roadless terrain and made it easier to bypass fortified areas like Mishan, which bristled with 420 pillboxes. Improvised cross-country roads allowed for tank movement in the advanced detachments, but could not support the follow-on rifle divisions, artillery, and motor transport without being torn up. To solve this problem, the 1st Red Banner Army, under a veteran of night warfare, General Beloborodov, built two or three roads per division over the taiga.

Beloborodov's troops had trained in mountain forests and swamps and had for several decades been stationed in taiga terrain on the Soviet side of the border. The general selected a tactical plan similar to one he had discussed with his present corps commanders during the conflict with the Japanese in 1938—39.[75] In June and July, the 35th Army had also conducted training exercises for battalions, regiments, and divisions on similar terrain. This training was particularly important because the 35th Army's main attack took place north of Lake Khanka, over swampy terrain that the Japanese considered impassable and thus not worthy of a major defensive effort. These tactics and training, combined with scrupulous security, elaborate deception techniques, torrential rain, and the cover of darkness, assured surprise. In the 25th Army area, the noise of the rain so effectively muffled the movement of the assault detachments that advanced battalions were launched two hours later at 0300. The remainder of the 25th Army and the main forces of other front armies, some of which would have to contend with more difficult terrain or stiffer Japanese resistance, would not attack until 0830, according to plan.[76]

Although considered of secondary importance to the deeper pincerlike thrusts of the Trans-Baikal and First Far Eastern Fronts, the efforts of the Second Far Eastern Front in northern Manchuria served to tie down some of the best prepared and hardest fighting Japanese forces. Its front-wide night attack at 0100 was noteworthy mainly because the Amur Naval Flotilla supported its assault on the Amur River islands. Thus, the 361st Division captured the island of Tatar near the mouth of the Sungari River on the night of the ninth and was equally effective against Fuchin on the night of the twelfth, though the Soviets did not take the city until later on the thirteenth. Naval flotilla gunboats supported both operations. In another night attack characteristic of Soviet command initiative, this time by elements of the 16th Army on Sakhalin island, the 79th Rifle Division commander led an entire regiment across a swamp, wading through waist-high water and appearing in the rear of Japanese fortifications while a frontal attack occupied the defenders. Before this determined initiative on the night of 13—14 August, the Soviet offensive had been stalled for two days. Other night attacks, such as the fierce day-night action at Mutanchiang, where the Japanese suffered heavy losses, might be cited as evidence of the effective employment of night operations by Soviet forces in the short, decisive Manchurian campaign. As the Soviets themselves gloated,

> darkness was a powerful ally that allowed the Soviet troops to ensure the continuity of their offensive and launch surprise attacks. The Japanese had boasted that night was their trump card, but all their attempts to achieve success at night came to nothing.[77]

On 23 August, Stalin announced the conclusion of the successful Manchurian campaign. A week and a half later, the Japanese signed the formal papers of surrender. World War II was over.

Conclusion

During World War II, the Soviets were not the only great power to employ successful night operations. The Germans had used night operations in Poland in 1939 to pursue the withdrawing Poles in order to achieve an operational advantage. Desert operations in North Africa often capitalized on darkness because daylight gave the defender substantial advantages. In the fighting from El Alamein to Tunis, every major attack began at night. Pursuit operations in Sicily continued around the clock. In Italy and France, the U.S. 3d Infantry Division adopted night operations as a standing operating procedure and developed considerable skill in execution. It distinguished night attacks from daylight attacks only by the degree of control required. Specially trained for night operations by its commander in the United States, the U.S. 104th Infantry Division launched more than 100 successful night attacks in Holland and Germany. The U.S. 30th Infantry Division had similar successes in France, Belgium, Holland, and Germany. The Germans used night operations in the east more and more as the odds turned against them and as the Russians forced them to fight at night. In the west, Allied air power and firepower forced a similar reversion to night operations on the part of the Germans.[78]

Thus night operations were not unique to the Soviets. Nor was the Soviet progression from night operations based almost entirely on stealth and cold steel to night operations based on speed, firepower, and aggressiveness unique. What was unique was that the Russians conducted night operations more often and on a larger scale than any of the other combatants in World War II. The Soviets' selective use of night operations enhanced their powerful reconnaissance in force, advanced detachment, and second echelon operations. By the latter stages of the war (1943—45), their operations reflected the considerable skill, training, and leadership they had developed. Although these operations were by no means universally successful, they took place, at least during the last three years of the war, in a framework of gradual, but inexorable movement westward. It might be argued that the Soviet drive to the west took on a progressively more relentless character as the Soviets gradually turned towards larger and more frequent operations at night.[79] An examination of the growth and success of Soviet night operations, however, reveals their dynamic nature and defies simple generalizations.

As might be expected by the ebb and flow of Soviet fortunes, the development of Soviet night operations during the war was uneven. The initial impetus for the increased use of night operations came from early successes in this tactic and the incentive provided by German command of the air. In the Moscow counteroffensive, the Military Council of the Western Front issued a special directive ordering "extensive surprise nighttime operations."[80] In practice, this order translated into small-scale actions with limited objectives. With the shifting of the strategic balance at Stalingrad, however, the Soviets began to consider night operations in terms of more ambitious offensives. By mid-1943, when the balance of manpower and equipment had definitely swung to their favor, the Soviets planned night operations on a larger scale in order to take advantage of the newfound mobility and offensive power of the tank army.

The increasing sophistication of German defenses and the desire to maintain relentless pressure on the withdrawing German forces impelled the Soviets to use night operations in response to specific and varying challenges. At Zaporozh'e, for example, the Russians resorted to night attacks when day attacks failed. (It was during this operation that the first Soviet front-level night attack took place.) Similarly, failure was the challenging circumstance that inspired the reversion to night operations in a later stage of the battle for the Dnieper. The inability to break out of the major bridgehead gained at Bukrin Bend resulted in the *Stavka* decision to transfer the 3d Guards Tank Army, the 7th Assault Artillery Corps, the 23d Infantry Corps, and other units north, under cover of darkness, to the smaller bridgehead at Lutezh. Apparently undetected in the 130- to 200-kilometer change of fronts, the units managed a successful breakout from Lutezh and a drive on to Kiev.[81] This operation featured a day-night attack, most noteworthy because of the introduction of second echelon elements from the tank army at the onset of darkness. This tactic became more prevalent in 1944—45.

Front-level night operations in 1944 tended to be more limited in scope than those of Zaporozh'e and Kiev in 1943. In 1944, the Soviets employed night attacks primarily to intensify pursuit, to reduce encirclements, and to cross major water barriers without undue delay or casualties. An increased reliance on night operations demonstrated the desire to achieve surprise and to grasp the initiative (always important considerations in the Russian approach to war). This was exemplified in the operations of the Third and Fourth Ukrainian Fronts in the south in spring 1944, when pouring rains and muddy roads enhanced surprise at night.

In 1945 when the Soviets were conducting the last great offensives of the war, the need to conserve manpower and to achieve surprise encouraged night operations. Under these circumstances, night operations continued to be important for reconnaissance in force, advanced detachment spearheads, and other forms of day-night offensive operations designed to keep the Germans off balance and to maintain combat pressure on them. The year began with the day-night efforts to reduce the German and Hungarian forces in the encircled Hungarian capital of Budapest and ended with the lightning campaign in Manchuria.[82] It also witnessed numerous and for the most part successful night engagements in the East Prussian and Vistula-Oder campaigns. Although these campaigns primarily involved the use of forward detachments in pursuit operations and the skillful introduction of second echelon forces at night, they also included operations as diverse as night attacks by Soviet horse cavalry on German lines of communication and night bombing of communication lines and cities. A long series of night bombing raids, for example, destroyed the city of Tilsit in East Prussia.[83]

The final months of the war also witnessed multifront operations before Berlin and in the Manchurian theater. At Berlin, Zhukov's front was less successful than that of Konev's, but they faced different circumstances and forces. Nonetheless, Zhukov has been justly criticized for his failure to conceal the buildup for this operation and for his failure to employ his reconnaissance in force battalions at night and closer to the time of the main attack in order to upset German expectations. On the other hand, perhaps profiting from these mistakes, Vasilevsky conducted amazingly successful night operations in Manchuria. Three widely separated fronts, with armies and divisions attacking in widely separated column formations, conducted an attack with the utmost secrecy, taking maximum advantage of bad weather and darkness. Night operations in the difficult mountain taiga terrain of Manchuria favored the highly mobile, fast-moving Soviet columns. The terrain seems to have slowed the Soviets only at Hailar, where their ambitious plans for a difficult, timed pincer movement by two widely separated forces proved too great a challenge. It is noteworthy that the Soviets chose not to employ airborne forces in Manchuria after the two disastrous night drops at Vyazma-Yukhnov (1942) and at the Dnieper Bend (1943). The Soviets did, however, make several combat air landings of small forces to seize key installations in the heart of Manchuria and Korea. They were eminently successful in gaining and maintaining the initiative and minimizing their casualties.

Although the Soviets at times suffered heavy casualties and even reverses at night, such as at Kharkov, this was more the exception than the rule. Most senior German officers who fought the Soviets on the Eastern Front acknowledged their "natural superiority in fighting during night, fog, rain or snow,"[84] and especially their skill in night infiltration tactics, reconnaissance, and troop movements and concentrations.[85] One German general said that the Soviets were driven to the concept of systematic infantry and armor attacks at night by the diminishing ability of the Germans to defend themselves; he admitted that the Soviet night attacks often succeeded.[86] Other German officers criticized the Soviets for failing, in 1944, to conceal night movements by dimming vehicle lights, but the magnitude of the surprise achieved in the Byelorussian campaign of that year indicates that the Soviets could and did conceal major troop movements most effectively when they deemed concealment critical.[87]

The success of Soviet night operations was in large part due to intensive training and the ability to profit from mistakes and failures. The Germans, who were sparing and hesitant in their compliments concerning Soviet military prowess were nonetheless compelled to acknowledge the Soviet ability to learn from their opponents.[88] High-level Soviet military planners constantly analyzed not only the Red Army's performance, but also that of the Germans, as in a chess match, to determine necessary corrective action. This type of analysis extended down to lower staffs (to army and perhaps division level).[89]

Although the Soviet combat leaders were acutely aware that "the success of any battle is determined in great measure by the extent of preparation,"[90] training standards for night operations were not uniform. Some units published special instructions for certain aspects of night operations, while others did not amplify the regulations.[91] This sort of unevenness should not be difficult to understand. Various American units, it might be noted, were also characterized by distinct, sometimes unique, standing operating procedures. In the war some American divisions were proficient in night operations, while others were not. Soviet training for night operations, at least in 1944—45 was, however, more widespread and intensive than that of comparable U.S. or German units.

During the period between major offensives, sometimes lasting weeks, the Soviets trained vigorously on terrain similar to that which they expected to encounter. Mockups and live fire enhanced realism in combined arms exercises. Training for breakthrough of a fortified area, for example, included command post exercises with maps and terrain models, followed by reconnaissance on the ground; it emphasized coordination with combined arms support, coordination with adjacent units, and the "display of daring and intelligent initiative."[92] The Committee for the Study of War Experiences of the General Staff issued a manual on breakthrough of fortified areas for the instruction of officers. It established centralized training at army or army group level, with periods of training and training sites specified for corps and division commanders charged with working out detailed programs. It also encouraged "bold, but reasonable initiative on the part of commanders."[93] Although there is no comparable document for training on night operations, one contemporary Soviet analyst contends that from mid-1943 on "virtually all regiments of the division" trained for night combat in order to maintain high operational tempos.[94] This seems essentially correct for units participating in the final offensives of the war. In the East Prussian Operation three battalions from each division trained specifically for night operations, and up to one-half of all training was at night. Other battalions trained for assault of a fortified zone, pursuit operations, and advanced detachment operations, all of which might and usually did involve night combat.[95] Published guidance in the field service regulations established a certain degree of uniformity, especially in command and control measures.

Although the Soviets have made a great effort to analyze the evolution and growth of night operations since the war, during the war they were probably not fully aware of how far these operations had permeated their tactics at all levels. Nonetheless, it is obvious that not all Soviet units were involved in night operations to the same extent, although day-night pursuit, river crossings, and reduction of encirclements at night were common. The 1944 Field Service Regulations, while describing night actions as "usual occurrences," nonetheless cautioned that plans should be simple in concept and limited in mission, with short, straight attack movements. Complicated maneuvers were still forbidden.[96] Shortly after the war, however, prominent military leaders noted that the excessive limitations of this regulation were outdated. In 1946, Colonel General Kuznetsov stated that "darkness does not interfere with the employment of any of the modern means of combat" and that "tactical experience has shown that there is no branch of the Army which cannot participate in night battles of all kinds."[97]

Contemporary Soviet commentators and analysts echo these sentiments. Night operations, they argue, are applicable to modern warfare. They cite three factors as being critical for success. The first concerns the amount of daylight hours allocated to preparation for a night attack. One Soviet survey of the wartime experience of sixteen rifle divisions in night attacks shows that they had had between two and fourteen hours of preparation, but only one to seven of those hours during daylight.[98] Limited daylight precludes reconnaissance of the terrain and makes planning difficult for junior commanders and staffs. The current Soviet objective is to allow enough time for daylight planning of night operations and to teach that night operations require more time to plan than comparable daylight operations.

The second factor is command and control, with which the Soviets displayed varying degrees of success during World War II. Their success at Zaporozh'e depended on control measures specified in the field service regulations as well as innovative use of white paint and signaling devices. Command and control at Berlin broke down after initial success when the use of searchlights and German countermeasures proved confusing. The Soviets apparently overcame these problems in Manchuria, however, where command and control proved excellent, despite the challenge of moving large units on widely dispersed, separate axes of advance over difficult terrain.

The Soviets have concluded that they overcame command and control problems during the war by

> bringing the command post closer to the troops, by establishing a rigid procedure for the moving up of the commander and the staff in time and according to the lines, by designating with code light signals the location of the command and observation posts, the message and communication centers, and by the positioning of staff officers in the units during the period of attack. Sound and light signals duplicated by radio were used for communications.[99]

The third issue of concern is that the "troops possess high moral qualities," which the Soviets interpret as moral courage and the will to win. The Soviets constantly refer to the educational propaganda of their political workers in every unit and in every campaign as having provided necessary psychological preparations for battle. These political workers wielded great influence and were effective in instilling hatred of an enemy whose capital was described in such colorful phrases as the "lair of the Fascist beast."[100] On the eve of major campaigns, they worked the troops into a rage of patriotic fervor, signing up thousands of men for the Communist party and its youth division, Komsomol. They also had heroic acts of party members publicized. Because successful night operations required psychological preparation as well as extensive field training, Soviet preeminence in night operations was possibly attributable, at least in part, to these party-controlled political workers.[101]

Finally, a discussion of Soviet night operations in World War II would be incomplete without reference to their impetus, their emphasis, and their future implications. To a certain extent the impetus for night operations came from Stalin and the *Stavka* itself, because strategy and, to some extent, tactics were developed, or at least approved, by Stalin personally or by *Stavka* representatives like Marshals Vasilevsky and Zhukov.[102] The function of *Stavka* representatives was to insure that front and multifront operations were coordinated at all levels and carried out with the requisite zeal, determination, and skill. Yet, despite the level of control by the Supreme Headquarters Command, front and army commanders were sometimes able to get the highest authority to bless *their own* strategic or operational plans, such as General Beloborodov's plan for a night attack to break the encirclement of the 43d Army during the Byelorussian campaign. In this case army commander Beloborodov suggested an unusual night attack led by tanks with headlights on and had it approved by both the front commander and the *Stavka* representative.[103] Top commanders were not afraid to experiment and tailor their operations to individual circumstances, particularly after 1943. As Soviet combat leaders gained more confidence after each victory over the Germans, this gradual process of experimenting and tailoring trickled down to lower level commanders, as the actions of Colonel Gusakovsky at Meseritz and the degree of responsibility placed on battalion commanders for reconnaissance in force and brigade commanders of advanced detachments, show. Only the most experienced officers were selected for this duty, according to General M. Y. Katukov, who commanded the 1st Guards Tank Army, from which Gusakovsky, twice hero of the Soviet Union, was chosen:

> Among combat units with excellent records it is the custom to designate as the commanders of forward elements and advance guards, as well as reconnaissance groups, officers who have distinguished themselves by their daring and capacity for decisive action.... Officers of the forward element recognize that the slightest manifestation of indecision on their part can result in failure of the tactical plans of their superior commander. They are called upon to demonstrate initiative, boldness and courage.[104]

Thus, despite centralized control, there was room for initiative and boldness. Generals Chuikov and Kuznetsov both wrote of the need to be daring at night. In a recent article, a former Soviet battalion and regimental commander in the war, General I. Tretyak, expressed the requirement for initiative in terms of the "method" developed by M. V. Frunze, a famous military leader of the Bolshevik Revolution:

> The essence of this method is that there cannot be anything absolute or ossified, everything flows and changes and any means, any method can find employment in a corresponding situation. The commander's skill is manifested by his ability to choose from a variety of means at his disposal the ones which will give the best results in a given situation.[105]

Tretyak goes on to refer to battle as a "struggle of brains, an intellectual clash with the enemy" and speaks of the need for the commander to be a person of "bold thinking and solid erudition."[106] General A. A. Luchinsky, who commanded the 28th Army in Europe and the 39th Army in Manchuria, where Soviet forces grasped the initiative and never relinquished it, recently observed that

> initiative frequently manifests itself in the fact that, without orders from above, a commander will decide independently to accomplish a general objective, even if it substantially differs from the senior commander's previously issued instructions, but conforms to his concept and the situation.[107]

To the Soviets, "creative employment of combat experience with due regard for weapons and equipment" is a watchword.[108] The emphasis in Russian night operations during the war—and as expressed in Soviet literature today—is on initiative, boldness, and daring, within the framework of the senior commander's concept. This is perfectly in consonance with the seven basic Soviet principles of operational art and tactics, particularly the principles of surprise, combat activeness and mobility, and high tempos of combat operations.

The Russians' predilection for night operations extending back at least to the late nineteenth century is perhaps not so significant as the skill the Red Army displayed in multifront, combined arms night operations in World War II; the way in which the wartime experience dramatically altered Soviet perceptions about what large combined arms units could accomplish at night;[109] and the emphasis Soviet military literature today places on the wartime successes in this area. (Recent Soviet literature tends to shed light on less than successful night operations as well.) The face of modern war changes at a maddening pace, but basic principles and successful methods of operation tend to endure. What is clear from this study is that night operations became an integral part of Soviet operations in general during World War II, a fact not lost on Soviet planners and commentators today, but one inexplicably overlooked in the West. (The U.S. Department of the Army "red book" titled *Soviet Army Operations* (1976) says almost nothing about night operations, but notes merely that the Soviet emphasis on high operational tempos implies combat on a twenty-four-hour basis.[110]) The Soviets recognize a variety of methods for achieving surprise and grasping the initiative by employing night operations; they are likely to be proficient in their use in any future conflict. Despite the current profusion of night vision devices that turn night into day, American military planners and officers, especially those studying the AirLand Battle, might be well advised to take note of the historical and modern emphasis the Russians place upon nighttime operations.

Appendix

Table of Soviet Night Operations, World War II

Name of Operation/ Battle (Date)	Location	Units Fighting	Type Operation	Depth of Penetration	Unique Features/Remarks
Moscow/Uzlovaya (18 Nov 41)	SE of Moscow	Rifle division of 10th Army	Infantry night attack	3 km	Tanks leading infantry.
Moscow/Vyazma (Jan-Feb 42)	Vyazma-Yukhnov	4th Airborne Corps	Airborne	N/A	Night drop behind enemy lines failed because of poor organization and execution.
Stalingrad (20-24 Aug 42)	Don River Bend	197th Rifle Division 14th Guards Rifle Division 203d Rifle Division	River crossing	N/A	Two divisions (followed by a third) crossed simultaneously on a 24-km front.
Stalingrad (19-23 Nov 42)[1]	Kalach on the Don River	26th Tank Corps	Encirclement	N/A	Russian tankers deceived the German defenders by seizing a linkup point in their rear area at night with headlights on.
Belgorod-Kharkov (3-23 Aug 43)	Kharkov	5th Guards Tank Army	Mass tank attack	N/A	Mass tank attacks against prepared defense failed to achieve desired result without effective air, artillery, or infantry support.
Liberation of Left Bank of Ukraine (22-30 Sep 43)	Dnieper River	Voronezh, Steppe, and Southwest Fronts	River crossing	N/A	Soviet army crossed major river (mostly at night) along a 750-km front with advanced detachments leading.
Liberation of Left Bank of Ukraine	Bukrin Bend on Dnieper	1st, 3d, and 5th Airborne Brigades	Airborne—to seize bridgehead	N/A	Night drop without reconnaissance led to disaster.
Zaporozh'e (12-14 Oct 43)	Zaporozh'e bridgehead	8th Guards Tank Army 12th Army 3d Guards Army	Combined arms	5-6 km (12-13 Oct) 8-10 km (13-14 Oct)	Separate army night attacks followed by a front-wide night attack preceded by artillery preparation. Tank and mechanized corps committed on the flanks of the breakthrough.

Table of Soviet Night Operations, World War II—Continued

Name of Operation/ Battle (Date)	Location	Units Fighting	Type Operation	Depth of Penetration	Unique Features/Remarks
Kiev (4-5 Nov 43)	Kiev	3d Guards Tank Army 38th Army	Combined arms night attack	7-8 km	Tanks passed through infantry in evening light and continued attack by night with sirens howling and lights on. Marked beginning of use of second echelons at night.
Korsun-Shevchenkovsky (16-17 Feb 44)	Shanderovka	Volunteer Komsomol pilots	Night bombing	N/A	Night bombing in bad weather assisted in defeating German attempts to break out of encirclement.
Bereznegovatoye-Snigirevka (6-7 Mar 44)	Southern Ukraine	Third Ukrainian Front	Pursuit	UNK	Cavalry-mechanized group used to pursue withdrawing forces over muddy terrain.
Crimean (10-11 Apr 44)	Kerch peninsula	51st Separate Coastal Army	Pursuit	70 km	Reconnaissance in force led army in night pursuit.
Byelorussia (27-29 Jun 44)	Bobruisk	65th Army	Preservation of encirclement (counterattack)	N/A	German efforts to break encirclement were frustrated by bombing and strafing of 500 attack planes, followed by combined arms ground attack.
Lublin-Brest (18-20 Jul 44)	East of Lublin	88th and 39th Rifle Divisions of 8th Guards Army	Combined arms night attack	4 km 5 km	Consecutive day-night attacks for two days and nights used second echelon forces. This mode of operation was repeated in the Vistula-Oder and East Prussian offensives of 1945.
Vistula-Oder (29-30 Jan 45)	Meseritz fortified area	44th Tank Bde of 11th Guards Tank Corps 1st Guards Tank Army	Night attack through fortified area	UNK	Breaching of fortified area at night on initiative of advanced detachment commander.
Berlin (15-16 Apr 45)	East and SE of Berlin	First Byelorussian Front First Ukrainian Front	Multifront night attack	3.5-4 km	Unprecedented artillery barrages followed by multifront night attacks. Searchlights used to blind defenders by night and smoke by day along a 390-km front (First Ukrainian Front).
Berlin (21 Apr-2 May 45)	Berlin	First Byelorussian Front Second Byelorussian Front First Ukrainian Front	MOUT (street fighting)	N/A	Lessons learned at Stalingrad, Poznan, and other cities led to systematic division of city in which night operations were reserved for difficult and important objectives.

Table of Soviet Night Operations, World War II—*Continued*

Name of Operation/Battle (Date)	Location	Units Fighting	Type Operation	Depth of Penetration	Unique Features/Remarks
Manchurian Campaign (9-10 Aug 45)	Manchurian borders	Trans-Baikal Front First Far Eastern Front Second Far Eastern Front	Theater-level night offensive	4-50 km	Unprecedented and extensive preparation to deceive the Japanese and achieve strategic as well as tactical surprise. Theater-level night attack with skillful blending of reconnaissance in force, assault detachments, advanced battalions, and advanced detachments. Almost no artillery or air preparation. Assault on Amur River islands supported by naval flotilla gunboats.
Sakhalin island (13-14 Aug 45)	Sakhalin island	79th Rifle Division	Divisional night attack	UNK	Two-front attack. Frontal attacks fixed defenders' attention while strike force maneuvered over "impassable" water obstacle to attack from rear. Reminiscent of similar successes at the isthmus of Perekop (Nov 1920) and at Viborg, Finland (1940).

Notes

Abbreviations used in the notes:

CARL — U.S. Army Command and General Staff College Combined Arms Research Library, followed by the document call number.
DTIC — Defense Technical Information Center, Defense Logistics Agency, Cameron Station, Alexandria, Virginia.
URMA — *USSR Report: Military Affairs*
VIZ — *Voyenno-Istoricheskiy Zhurnal* [Military history journal]

1. "Night Combat," *Military Review* 24 (February 1948):81, translated and digested from an article in *Revista de la Oficialidad de Complemento, Apendice de la Revista Ejercito* (Spain), May 1947.
2. The storming of Kars and Erzerum, the capture of Ft. Hafiz, and the battle of Shipka were examples of Russian night operations that captured the attention of the European press of that day. *Night Fighting,* 2d ed. (London: William Clowes and Sons, 1893), p. 9, photocopy of published pamphlet containing translation of article from *Svoennei Sbornik* [Russian military magazine], December 1885, CARL 355.422 S968n2.
3. Gorman C. Smith, "Division Night Attack Doctrine" (Master's thesis, U.S. Army Command and General Staff College, 1964), pp. 80—81.
4. Guenther Blumentritt, "Operations in Darkness and Smoke," draft translation by A. Schroeder, mimeographed (U.S. Army, Europe, Historical Division, 1952), pp. 4, 19, MS B-683, CARL N17785.
5. V. Panov, "The Great Patriotic War and Postwar Period," *URMA,* no. 1557 (16 January 1981):68, JPRS 77187, translated by the Foreign Broadcast Information Service from the Russian article in *VIZ,* October 1980.
6. V. Kuznetsov, "Night Actions," pp. 2—3, translated by the AC of S, G-2, U.S. Army, Historical Division, European Command, from an article in *Voyennyi Vestnik* [Military Herald], no. 9, 1946.
7. Alan Clark, *Barbarossa: The Russian-German Conflict, 1941-45* (New York: William Morrow and Co., 1965), p. 89.
8. Albert Kesselring et al., "Night Combat," mimeographed (Karlsruhe, Germany: Historical Division, U.S. Army European Command, July 1952), p. 7, MS P-054a, CARL N17500.17A.
9. M. Lukin, "In the Vyaz'ma Operation," *URMA,* no. 1643 (7 January 1982):35—45, JPRS 79812, translated by the Foreign Broadcast Information Service from the Russian article in *VIZ,* September 1981.
10. Kesselring, "Night Combat," p. 7.
11. "Peculiarities of Russian Warfare," rev. ed., mimeographed (U.S. Army, Historical Division, June 1949), pp. 141—43, MS T-22, CARL N16276 (hereafter cited as "Peculiarities").
12. Heinz Guderian, *Panzer Leader,* translated from the German by Constantine Fitzgibbon (New York: Ballantine Books, 1972, c1965), p. 190.

13. "Peculiarities," pp. 141—43.
14. Panov, "Great Patriotic War," p. 61. The Soviets used submachine gunners to lead night attacks, thus creating the impression that their forces were larger than they actually were.
15. Blumentritt, "Operations in Darkness and Smoke," pp. 21—22.
16. Yo Sukhinin, "Combat Action of Rifle Divisions at Night," translated by Lt. Col. David M. Glantz from the Russian article in *VIZ*, December 1977, pp. 50—51. Russian night attacks were not, of course, always successful. Although the Russians encircled 4,000 Germans at Cholm during the winter of 1941—42, they were not able to destroy them because their pattern of day and night attacks (128 in 105 days) was too predictable. This allowed the Germans sufficient time to shift forces within their perimeter and eventually to break out. See James Sidney Lucas, *War on the Eastern Front: The German Soldier in Russia* (New York: Stein and Day, 1979), pp. 196—205.
17. I. I. Lisov, *Parachutists—Airborne Landing*, translated for the U.S. Army Foreign Science and Technology Center by ACSI (1968; Washington, DC, 10 December 1969), pp. 84—139, DTIC AD 700943.
18. Blumentritt, "Operations in Darkness and Smoke," pp. 1—2.
19. There were, of course, German officers who maintained that their troops were more resistant to "the psychic effects of night" and that the Russian flanks were vulnerable to surprise at night. Kesselring, "Night Combat," pp. 1—3. According to Kesselring, German combat tactics, which were dependent upon the "initiative of lower echelon commanders," were hindered at night by an inability to recognize important defensive positions or accurately adjust fire. Ibid., p. v.
20. Department of Research into and Application of Wartime Experience, General Staff of the Red Army, *Collection of Materials for the Study of War Experience*, no. 8, August—October 1942 (Moscow, 1943), translated by the Directorate of Military Intelligence, Canadian Army Headquarters, Ottawa, 30 November 1955, pp. 126—29, CARL N16582.178-B. The authors considered the lack of air cover and feigned crossing sites as the main shortcomings of this operation. Ibid., p. 131. Kuznetsov, "Night Actions," p. 5, says this operation forced the Germans to divert three infantry divisions away from the drive on Stalingrad.
21. Panov, "Great Patriotic War," p. 66.
22. Peter Ribakov, "Soviet Night Attacks with Tanks," *The Cavalry Journal* 54 (May—June 1945):65.
23. Friedrich Wilhelm von Mellenthin, *Panzer Battles*, translated by H. Betzler (New York: Ballantine Books, 1971), p. 237. Almost a year to the day before this battle the Soviets had used an enveloping attack at night to take Chern in the Moscow offensive. Guderian, *Panzer Leader*, p. 209.
24. Amazasp Babadjanyan, "Tank and Mechanized Forces," in *The Battle of Kursk*, pp. 176—86 (Moscow: Progress Publishers, 1974), reprinted in P312 *Offensive Tactics Advance Sheets* (Fort Leavenworth, KS: U.S. Army Command and General Staff College, June 1981), pp. 194—95. The 1st Tank and 5th Guards Tank Armies, with about 800 vehicles each, acted as an armored wedge "to press home the attack in operational depth." Ibid.
25. "Peculiarities," pp. 92—97; Paul Karl Schmidt [Paul Carell], *Scorched Earth: The Russian-German War, 1943—1944* (New York: Ballantine Books, 1973), pp. 356—59. During this operation the Russians infiltrated by night a motorized infantry unit of about battalion strength into the German artillery position at Lyubotin, west of Kharkov. The next day the Germans discovered the unit and destroyed it. See "Peculiarities," p. 95.
26. Mellenthin, *Panzer Battles*, pp. 289—90.
27. Z. Alexandrov, "Night Attack," *Soviet Military Review*, August 1978, p. 48.
28. P. Milovanov, "Crossing the Dnieper," *Military Review* 24 (June 1944):111—13, translated from a Russian article in *Krasnaya Zvezda* [Red Star], 17 November 1943; Alexander Werth, *Russia at War, 1941—1945* (New York: E. P. Dutton and Co., 1964), pp. 773—74.
29. Mellenthin, *Panzer Battles*, p. 223. Russian river crossing techniques ignored the German principle of *Schwerpunkt* or "main blow" and instead advocated what Liddell Hart referred to as a "dispersed advance with distributed aim, i.e., against a number of objects simultaneously." On the Dnieper it was a case of dispersed attacks on a wide front that

triumphed over a concentrated defense, which although mobile, could not always be shifted in time to meet threats too numerous for the reserves to deal with. W. R. Young, "Russian Strategy and Tactics," *Military Review* 24 (March 1945):122, digested from an article in *The Fighting Forces* (Great Britain), 1944.

30. Lisov, *Parachutists*, pp. 140—52. See Schmidt, *Scorched Earth*, pp. 407—11, whose account, based mostly on captured German sources, is also interesting, but not entirely accurate. He correctly points out that the Russians pioneered airborne operations with their exercises in the Caucasus in 1932 and quotes a Soviet marshal who expressed sadness that these paratroops were employed without "practicable plans."
31. Lisov, *Parachutists*, pp. 150—63; Sergei Matveevich Shtemenko, *The Soviet General Staff at War (1941—1945)* (Moscow: Progress Publishers, 1970), pp. 185—87.
32. A. Zvenzlovsky, "Night Attack," *Soviet Military Review*, May 1973, pp. 50—52; Vasilii Ivanovich Chuikov, *V Boyakh Za Ukrainu* [In the Battle for the Ukraine] (Kiev: Izdatel'stvo Politcheskoi Litertury Ukrainy, 1972), pp. 81—108, translated by Lt. Col. David M. Glantz; Sukhinin, "Combat Action," pp. 50—51.
33. Chuikov, "Street Fighting—The Lessons of Stalingrad," *Military Review* 24 (October 1944): 98—99, digested from an article in *An Cosantoir* (Ireland), March 1944, that was reprinted from Chuikov's *The Epic Story of Stalingrad* (London: Hutchinson & Co., n.d.). Chuikov's 62d Army at Stalingrad was later renamed 8th Guards Army. In June 1943 his staff had issued a special order on using light signals in night operations (Panov, "Great Patriotic War," p. 64).
34. Chuikov, "Street Fighting," pp. 98—99; Panov, "Great Patriotic War," p. 67; Alexandrov, "Night Attack," p. 48.
35. Schmidt, *Scorched Earth*, pp. 424—27; Panov, "Great Patriotic War," p. 65.
36. Sukhinin, "Combat Action," p. 51.
37. John Erickson, "Soviet Combined—Arms: Theory and Practice," photocopy of typescript (Edinburgh, Scotland: University of Edinburgh, September 1979), p. 51. Soviet authors do not attempt to quantify their night operations, but seek rather to explain the transition in the words of a former German General Staff officer, General Middledorf, who wrote: "Late in 1943 the Russians drew correct conclusions from their rich experience in night operations. They started to launch offensives at night, usually setting the forces' missions to a considerable depth. They used large tank forces to fulfill these missions and this often brought them success." See Z. Shutov, "Night Operations," *Soviet Military Review*, September 1981, p. 36; Panov, "Great Patriotic War," p. 68.
38. N. Kobrin, "Encirclement Operations," *Soviet Military Review*, August 1981, p. 38. German accounts refer to this encirclement as the Cherkassy pocket, although the city of Cherkassy was not in the pocket.
39. Werth, *Russia at War*, pp. 778—81. Russian accounts indicate that the Germans were unsuccessful at breaking the encirclement and claim 55,000 German casualties and 18,000 prisoners. German accounts acknowledge 20,000 men captured or killed, but claim that 30,000 or more escaped.
40. Alexandrov, "Night Attack," p. 49.
41. Shutov, "Night Operations," p. 36.
42. The reconnaissance in force (also referred to as reconnaissance in strength) was an important means of determining precise enemy locations and was sufficiently varied to confuse the Germans as to exact timing of Soviet offensives. Because the Germans, at this stage in the war, had the habit of withdrawing into the depths of their defenses to avoid the devastating Soviet artillery preparation, the reconnaissance in strength was often a key to Soviet success. This was the case in the Lvov-Sandomir Operation (July—August 1944), in which a Soviet reconnaissance in strength conducted at night discovered that the Germans were withdrawing from their first line of defenses. See A. Popov, "Reconnaissance in Strength," *Soviet Military Review*, March 1979, pp. 39—41.
43. Kuznetsov, "Night Actions," p. 4.
44. S. Shishkin, "The Vitebsk Operation," *Military Review* 25 (July 1945):96—97, translated from a Russian article in *Krasnaya Zvezda* [Red Star], 25 October 1944.
45. P. Boldyrev, "The Bobruisk Operation," *Military Review* 24 (March 1945):105—8, translated and digested from a Russian article in *Krasnaya Zvezda* [Red Star], 28 September 1944.

46. Apparently unaware of a similar attack earlier at Kiev, Beloborodov expressed his appreciation in a recent interview to his former commanders for approving his innovative and successful tactic. A. P. Beloborodov, "About Some Military Leaders" (Interview), *Soviet Military Review*, July 1981, pp. 49—51.
47. Sukhinin, "Combat Action," p. 51.
48. Evidences of Soviet specialized training extend back at least as far as the campaigns in the Ukraine in 1943, where one Soviet division trained special destroyer battalions for reconnaissance and surprise attacks on strongpoints. A night attack by one of these destroyer battalions on the village of Khotomlya succeeded in routing a garrison of 700 men from the German 294th Infantry Division, but only because the signal for the attack (a red flare) was given by a German sentry, who was employing the flare because he had detected Soviet troops crawling towards his position. See Captain Sokolsky, "Night Raid on the Village of Khotomlya," *Military Review* 24 (June 1944):93—95, translated from *Voyennyi Vestnik* [Military Herald], June 1943.
49. The advanced detachments of the 11th Guards Army conducted five night exercises before their participation in the East Prussian campaign, while the 3d Guards Tank Army conducted half of its exercises at night before the Vistula-Oder operation, according to Panov, "Great Patriotic War," pp. 64—66.
50. K. Galitsky, "Certain Problems Pertaining to Breakthrough of Position Defenses," translated by the AC of S, G-2, Department of the Army, from *Voyennyi Vestnik* [Military Herald], October 1945, p. 10, CARL N18603.26; Panov, "Great Patriotic War," p. 65; Sukhinin, "Combat Action," pp. 51—52.
51. Panov, "Great Patriotic War," p. 66.
52. M. Y. Katukov, *Spearhead of the Main Effort* (Moscow: Military Publishing House, 1974), excerpts reprinted in *Soviet Military Review*, special supplement, September 1976, pp. 14—15.
53. Ibid., pp. 15—16. Because of the interrogation of German prisoners captured in the area by a patrol of the 1st Guards Tank Army on 26 January, the Soviets knew that many sectors of the line at Meseritz were not yet manned. See Otto Preston Chaney, *Zhukov* (Norman: University of Oklahoma Press, 1971), p. 298.
54. A good discussion on the controversy concerning the halt in February may be found in Chaney, *Zhukov*, pp. 300—306, where he also points out Zhukov's genuine concern and insight regarding the threat to his north from German forces in Pomerania. For another view, see Chuikov, *The Fall of Berlin*, translated from the German by Ruth Kisch (New York: Holt, Rinehart and Winston, 1967), pp. 116—22.
55. Normally used in the air defense role, searchlights were also employed against a German division in the mountains of Italy in 1944 by Americans attempting to restrict the unit's movement at night. Albert Kesselring et al., "Night Combat: Project #40," typescript (U.S. Army, Historical Division, European Command, April 1950), p. 61, MS P-0546, CARL N17500.17-B.
56. The reconnaissance was probably confined to the first and possibly second line of defenses in a defense in depth that extended back some thirty to forty kilometers. General Chuikov indicated his dissatisfaction with the information obtained on the "Nazi defense system, the grouping of forces, [and] the disposition of reserves." See Chuikov, *The Fall of Berlin*, p. 171.
57. Kuznetsov, "Night Actions," pp. 5—6.
58. Chaney, *Zhukov*, pp. 307—8, discusses the competition between the two marshals. The role of the Second Byelorussian Front north of the city should also be noted.
59. Andrew Tully, *Berlin, Story of a Battle* (1963; reprint ed., Westport, CT: Greenwood Press, 1977), p. 81. According to Tully the Soviets fired 41,600 cannon and rocket launchers along a 250-mile front. Shutov, "Night Operations," p. 36, said there were 325 guns per square kilometer of frontage.
60. *Reprints from the Soviet Press*, 30 April 1975, pp. 25—34, quoted in C. M. Flannery, "Night Operations—The Soviet Approach" (Master's thesis, U.S. Army Command and General Staff College, 1978), p. 14.
61. Chuikov, *The Fall of Berlin*, pp. 147—51; Chaney, *Zhukov*, p. 312; Sukhinin, "Combat Action," p. 52.

62. Vasily Yezhakov, "The Berlin Operation," *Soviet Military Review*, April 1975, p. 44; Chaney, *Zhukov*, pp. 312—16.
63. Kuznetsov, "Night Actions," p. 9. Guards mortars are multiple-rocket launchers.
64. "Red Army Field Service Regulations, 1944," mimeographed, translated by the AC of S, G-2, Department of the Army, 1952, p. 66. The regulation states that the "chief requisites for the success of the attack" include "strict secrecy as to the approaching attack, concealed concentration and movement of the troops into the jump-off position and surprise attack . . . . " This was not accomplished in the regrouping of eighteen Soviet armies, fifteen of which were moved a distance of about 365 kilometers and three of which were moved between 530 and 800 kilometers. See V. Kiselev, "Documents and Materials on the 35th Anniversary of the Berlin Operation," *URMA*, no. 1532 (10 September 1980):76, JPRS 76399, translated by the Foreign Broadcast Information Service from the Russian article in *VIZ*, May 1980.
65. Chuikov, *The Fall of Berlin*, pp. 143—44, notes both deficiencies but points out that secretive movement of tanks and artillery into their starting positions was not possible because of skillful employment of searchlights by the Germans on the Seelow Heights and of flares dropped from aircraft to illuminate the valley. This does not explain, however, why concealment was not maintained during the buildup for the general offensive.
66. Upon reaching the Memel and the Vistula in early 1945 after a five-week campaign, the Soviets had covered 435 miles at a blitzkrieg tempo that matched Guderian's and Hoth's pace along the Brest-Smolensk-Yelnya road in 1941. Schmidt, *Scorched Earth*, p. 596.
67. S. P. Ivanov, ed., *Nachal'nyi period voiny* [The initial phase of war] (Moscow: Voenizdat, 1974), pp. 282—83, quoted in Lilita I. Dzirkals, *"Lightning War" in Manchuria: Soviet Military Analysis of the 1945 Far East Campaign* (Santa Monica, CA: The Rand Corporation, January 1976), p. 5. The campaign was particularly time sensitive to the Soviets because they wanted their victory to be completed before America forced Japan out of the war. The first use of the atomic bomb on 6 August 1945 heightened this sensitivity.
68. M. V. Zakharov, ed., *Finale*, translated by David Skvirsky (Moscow: Progress Publishers, 1972), pp. 70—75. The Soviets employed "2,500,000 effectives, over 42,000 guns and mortars, over 6200 tanks and SPGs and 8300 combat aircraft" in the Berlin operation (Yezhakov, "The Berlin Operation," p. 42).
69. David M. Glantz, "Soviet Operations in Manchuria, August 1945," typescript (Fort Leavenworth, KS: Combat Studies Institute, U.S. Army Command and General Staff College, 1982), pt. 4, pp. 5—9.
70. Zakharov, *Finale*, pp. 102—3; Dzirkals, *"Lightning War,"* p. 41.
71. Dzirkals, *"Lightning War,"* pp. 128—29; Glantz, "Soviet Operations," pt. 2, p. 2. Reinforcements to the 6th Guards Tank Army converted it to a mechanized army consisting of forty-four motorized infantry battalions and twenty-five tank battalions. John Despres, Lilita Dzirkals, and Barton Whaley, *Timely Lessons of History: The Manchurian Model for Soviet Strategy* (Santa Monica, CA: The Rand Corporation, July 1976), p. 46, DTIC ADA 028881.
72. *Istoriia Vtoroi Mirovoi Voiny, 1939—1945* [History of the Second World War, 1939—1945], 12 vols. (Moscow: Voennoe Izdatel'stvo, 1972—), 11:5, 10—12, translated under contract by the U.S. government; Alexsandr A. Luchinskiy, "The Transbaikal Troops in the Hills of Manchuria," translated under contract by the U.S. government from the Russian article in *VIZ*, August 1971, pp. 7—8.
73. Zakharov, *Finale*, pp. 135—38; Dzirkals, *"Lightning War,"* p. 52; Historical Evaluation and Research Organization, *A Study of Breakthrough Operations* (Dunn Loring, VA, October 1976), p. 80. Zakharov, p. 92, states that GHQ had originally planned to use searchlights but canceled the idea after exercises showed this impractical in heavily wooded, mountainous terrain. Nonetheless, Marshal Meretskov was apparently prepared to use them.
74. K. Kalashnikov, "Memoirs: On the Far Eastern Borders," *URMA*, no. 1549 (8 December 1980):60—61, JPRS 76953, translated by the Foreign Broadcast Information Service from the Russian article in *VIZ*, August 1980; N. Tsygankov, "Certain Features of Combat Operations of the 5th Army in the Harbin-Kirin Operation," translated under contract by the U.S. government from the Russian article in *VIZ*, August 1975. As an exception, the 35th Army employed an artillery preparation against the Hutou fortified area.

75. A. P. Beloborodov, "In the Hills of Manchuria," *URMA*, no. 1587 (4 May 1981):104—9, JPRS 77987, translated by the Foreign Broadcast Information Service from the Russian article in *VIZ*, December 1980.
76. S. Pechenenko, "An Army Offensive Under Conditions of the Far Eastern Theater of Military Operations," *VIZ*, August 1978, pp. 42—49, translated under contract by the U.S. government; Glantz, "Soviet Operations in Manchuria," pt. 9, pp. 7—10.
77. Zakharov, *Finale*, pp. 144—45, 171—72.
78. W. D. Duncan, "Tanks and Infantry in Night Attacks," *Military Review* 27 (October 1947):46—47; Smith, "Division Night Attack Doctrine," pp. 88—109. Duncan also notes that the Japanese used night penetrations and infiltrations against inexperienced U.S. units during the first years of the war. Americans in the Pacific adopted the use of night attacks against strongpoints when the Japanese began to withdraw the bulk of their forces at night to avoid U.S. artillery fire.
79. The pace of Soviet operations was particularly intense in mid-1945, when the Soviets had their eyes trained on both the Americans and the Manchurian theater, which they wanted to open as soon as possible. In his drive on Prague, for example, Marshal Konev demanded a faster rate of advance from his army commanders despite the fact that his forces had advanced from ten to twenty-three kilometers on the night of 6—7 May 1945. Infantry and tanks were separated and given twenty-four-hour objectives of thirty to forty-five kilometers and fifty to sixty kilometers, respectively. On the night of 8—9 May, two of his tank armies covered eighty kilometers, bypassing obstacles and ignoring fatigue, in order to reach the Czechoslovakian capital. See I. Konev, "The Prague Operation," *Soviet Military Review*, May 1975, pp. 47—49.
80. Panov, "Great Patriotic War," p. 61.
81. K. Moskalenko, "Offensive from Lutezh Bridgehead," *Soviet Military Review*, September 1966, pp. 41—44.
82. S. Shtemenko, "General Staff During the War," *Soviet Military Review*, September 1974, p. 61.
83. See Nicolai Kostrov, "Soviet Night Attacks: Cavalry—1945," *The Cavalry Journal* 54 (May—June 1945):64, for a discussion of the use of Soviet cavalry in 1945; U.S. Department of the Army, Pamphlet no. 20—230: *Russian Combat Methods in World War II* (November 1950; reprint ed., Washington, DC, 1982), pp. 100—102, for the German view on the effectiveness of the Russian air force.
84. Max Simon, Generalleutnant Waffen SS, quoted in Kesselring, "Night Combat: Project #40," p. 59.
85. Kesselring, "Night Combat," pp. 2—5.
86. Curt Gallenkamp, quoted in Kesselring, "Night Combat: Project #40," p. 91.
87. The Soviet command concentrated 1,400,000 men for this campaign, but left four of the six Soviet tank armies on the southern wing of the front, thus deceiving the Germans into expecting a major blow farther to the south. See P. I. Batov, "The Blow in Byelorussia," *Soviet Military Review*, June 1979, pp. 6—9.
88. See, for example, Kesselring, "Night Combat," p. 6. The Russians are complimented for adapting their defensive tactics and techniques at night "to the more mobile and versatile German methods" by 1944.
89. Panov, "Great Patriotic War," p. 64.
90. A. Sazhin, "Breakthrough of a Fortified Region of the Enemy," p. 9, translated from *Voyennyi Vestnik* [Military Herald], 1944.
91. Panov, "Great Patriotic War," pp. 64—65.
92. Sazhin, "Breakthrough," p. 14.
93. General Staff of the Red Army, "Soviet Manual on Breakthrough of Fortified Areas," mimeographed 1944 translation by the AC of S, G-2, GSUSA, of the Soviet field regulation (Moscow: Military Publishing House of the People's Commissariat of Defense, 1944), pp. 19, 30, CARL R16582.105.
94. Sukhinin, "Combat Action," p. 52.
95. Galitsky, "Certain Problems," p. 10.
96. "Red Army Field Service Regulations, 1944," p. 134.
97. Kuznetsov, "Night Actions," p. 1.

98. Panov, "Great Patriotic War," p. 63.
99. Ibid., p. 67.
100. Sazhin, "Breakthrough," p. 22.
101. Almost all Soviet works on military history have at least a paragraph devoted to the role of political workers in preparing the troops for battle. See, for example, Batov, "The Blow in Byelorussia," p. 7. Although this is certainly propaganda, the role of such workers in preparing troops psychologically to fight at night cannot be discounted. Among the more famous party political workers in the army in the war were Nikita Khrushchev and Leonid Brezhnev.
102. The fact is evident in almost any Soviet work on the war, but a particularly good discussion of this is in M. Kozlov, "The Organization and Conduct of Strategic Defenses from the Experiences of the Great Patriotic War," *URMA*, no. 1587 (4 May 1981):31, JPRS 77987, translated by the Foreign Broadcast Information Service from the Russian article in *VIZ*, December 1980.
103. Similarly, in Manchuria, Beloborodov in conjunction with his corps commanders had his plans drawn up and approved by the front and theater commanders before the start of the operation. See Beloborodov, "Hills of Manchuria," pp. 108—9.
104. M. Y. Katukov, "The Armored Brigade in the Forward Element," translated by the Eurasian Branch, Historical Division, U.S. Army from *Zhurnal Bronetankovykh i Mekhanizirovannykh Voisk* [Journal of armored and mechanized troops], 1945.
105. I. Tretyak, "The Commander's Creative Activity," *URMA*, no. 1587 (4 May 1981):38, JPRS 77987, reprinted from *Soviet Military Review*, August 1980.
106. Ibid., p. 39. Panov, "Great Patriotic War," p. 66. expresses the same thoughts:
    The use of unusual methods for conducting combat operations and the manifestation of troop boldness and daring are an important factor in achieving success in nighttime combat. Under present-day conditions this also obliges us to carry out an active creative search for the most effective methods of the combat employment of the troops . . . .
107. Aleksandr A. Luchinskiy, "Initiative in Combat—Problems in Education: Front-Line Veterans on Their Combat Experience," *URMA*, no. 1638 (December 1981):2, JPRS 79602, translated by the Foreign Broadcast Information Service from the Russian article in *VIZ*, August 1981.
108. Sukhinin, "Combat Action," p. 52.
109. Sukhinin, "Combat Action," p. 52, for example, notes that in the later stages of the war Soviet divisions were assigned night objectives that were four to six kilometers or more in depth, thus corresponding to "close daylight objectives."
110. *Soviet Army Operations* (Arlington, VA: U.S. Department of the Army, Intelligence and Security Command, Threat and Analysis Center, April 1978), pp. 3—14.

Bibliography

Alexandrov, Z. "Night Attack." *Soviet Military Review,* August 1978, pp. 47—49.

Babadjanyan, Amazasp. "Tank and Mechanized Forces." In *The Battle of Kursk,* pp. 176—86. Moscow: Progress Publishers, 1974. Reprinted in P312 *Offensive Tactics Advance Sheets,* pp. 189—99. Fort Leavenworth, KS: U.S. Army Command and General Staff College, June 1981.

Batov, P. I. "The Blow in Byelorussia." *Soviet Military Review,* June 1979, pp. 6—9.

Beloborodov, A. P. "About Some Military Leaders." (Interview). *Soviet Military Review,* July 1981, pp. 49—51.

——— . "In the Hills of Manchuria." *USSR Report: Military Affairs,* no. 1587 (4 May 1981):104—11. JPRS 77987. Translated by the Foreign Broadcast Information Service from the Russian article in *Voyenno-Istoricheskiy Zhurnal* [Military history journal], December 1980.

Blumentritt, Guenther. "Operations in Darkness and Smoke." Draft translation by A. Schroeder. Mimeographed. U.S. Army, Europe, Historical Division, 1952. MS B-683. CARL N17785.

Boldyrev, P. "The Bobruisk Operation." *Military Review* 24 (March 1945): 105—8. Translated and digested from a Russian article in *Krasnaya Zvezda* [Red Star], 28 September 1944.

Chaney, Otto Preston. *Zhukov.* Norman: University of Oklahoma Press, 1971.

Chuikov, Vasilii Ivanovich. *The Fall of Berlin.* Translated from the Russian by Ruth Kisch. New York: Holt, Rinehart and Winston, 1967.

——— . "Street Fighting—The Lessons of Stalingrad." *Military Review* 24 (July 1944):95—99. Digested from an article in *An Cosantoir* (Ireland), March 1944, that was reprinted from Chuikov's *The Epic Story of Stalingrad* (London: Hutchinson & Co., n.d.).

——— . *V Boyakh Za Ukrainu* [In the battle for the Ukraine]. Kiev: Izdatel'stvo Politcheskoi Litertury Ukrainy, 1972. Translation of pp. 81—108 by Lt. Col. David M. Glantz.

Clark, Alan. *Barbarossa: The Russian-German Conflict, 1941—1945.* New York: William Morrow and Co., 1965.

Department of Research into and Application of Wartime Experience, General Staff of the Red Army. *Collection of Materials for the Study of War Experience,* no. 8, August—October 1942. Moscow, 1943. Translated by the Directorate of Military Intelligence, Canadian Army Headquarters, Ottawa, 30 November 1955. CARL N16582.178-B.

Despres, John; Dzirkals, Lilita; and Whaley, Barton. *Timely Lessons of History: The Manchurian Model for Soviet Strategy.* Santa Monica, CA: The Rand Corporation, July 1976. DTIC ADA 028881.

Duncan, W. D. "Tanks and Infantry in Night Attacks." *Military Review* 27 (October 1947):46—56.

Dzirkals, Lilita I. *"Lightning War" in Manchuria: Soviet Military Analysis of the 1945 Far East Campaign.* Santa Monica, CA: The Rand Corporation, January 1976. CARL N17074.2261.

Erickson, John. "Soviet Combined-Arms: Theory and Practice." Photocopy of typescript. Edinburgh, Scotland: University of Edinburgh, September 1979.

Flannery, C. M. "Night Operations—The Soviet Approach." Master's thesis, U.S. Army Command and General Staff College, 1978.

Galitsky, K. "Certain Problems Pertaining to Breakthrough of Position Defenses." Translated by AC of S, G-2, Department of the Army, from *Voyennyi Vestnik* [Military Herald], October 1945, pp. 1—10. CARL N18603.26.

General Staff of the Red Army. "Soviet Manual on Breakthrough of Fortified Areas." Mimeographed 1944 translation by AC of S, G-2, GSUSA, of the Soviet field regulation. Moscow: Military Publishing House of the People's Commissariat of Defense, 1944. CARL R16582.105.

Glantz, David M. "Soviet Operations in Manchuria, August 1945." Typescript. Fort Leavenworth, KS: Combat Studies Institute, U.S. Army Command and General Staff College, 1982.

Guderian, Heinz. *Panzer Leader.* Translated from the German by Constantine Fitzgibbon. New York: Ballantine Books, 1972, c1965.

Historical Evaluation and Research Organization. *A Study of Breakthrough Operations.* Dunn Loring, VA, October 1976.

Istoriia Vtoroi Mirovoi Voiny, 1939—1945 [History of the Second World War, 1939—1945]. Moscow: Voennoe Izdatel'stvo, 1980. Translated under contract by the U.S. government.

Kalashnikov, K. "Memoirs: On the Far Eastern Borders." *USSR Report: Military Affairs,* no. 1549 (8 December 1980):57—66. JPRS 76953. Translated by the Foreign Broadcast Information Service from the Russian article in *Voyenno-Istoricheskiy Zhurnal* [Military history journal], August 1980.

Katukov, M. Y. "The Armored Brigade in the Forward Element." Translated by the Eurasian Branch, Historical Division, U.S. Army, from *Zhurnal Bronetankovykh i Mekhanizirovannykh Voisk* [Journal of armored and mechanized troops], 1945.

_____. *Spearhead of the Main Effort.* Moscow: Military Publishing House, 1974. Excerpts reprinted in *Soviet Military Review,* special supplement, September 1976.

Kesselring, Albert, et al. "Night Combat." Mimeographed. Karlsruhe, Germany: Historical Division, U.S. Army European Command, July 1952. MS P-054a. CARL N17500.17A.

──── . "Night Combat: Project #40." Typescript. U.S. Army, Historical Division, European Command, April 1950. MS P-054b. CARL N17500.17-B. This document was combined with the one above and published as U.S. Department of the Army Pamphlet no. 20—236, *Night Combat,* in June 1953. The pamphlet was reprinted in June 1982.

Kiselev, V. "Documents and Materials on the 35th Anniversary of the Berlin Operation." *USSR Report: Military Affairs,* no. 1532 (10 September 1980):76—80. JPRS 76399. Translated by the Foreign Broadcast Information Service from the Russian article in *Voyenno-Istoricheskiy Zhurnal* [Military history journal], May 1980.

Kobrin, N. "Encirclement Operations." *Soviet Military Review,* August 1981, pp. 36—39.

Konev, I. "The Prague Operation." *Soviet Military Review,* May 1975, pp. 46—49.

Kostrov, Nicolai. "Soviet Night Attacks: Cavalry—1945." *The Cavalry Journal* 54 (May—June 1945):64—65.

Kuznetsov, V. "Night Actions." Translated by the AC of S, G-2, U.S. Army, Historical Division, European Command, from an article in *Voyennyi Vestnik* [Military Herald], no. 9, 1946.

Lisov, I. I. *Parachutists-Airborne Landing.* 1968. Translated for the U.S. Army Foreign Science and Technology Center by ACSI. Washington, DC, 10 December 1969. DTIC AD 700943.

Lucas, James Sidney. *War on the Eastern Front, 1941—1945: The German Soldier in Russia.* New York: Stein and Day, 1979.

Luchinskiy, Alexsandr A. "Initiative in Combat—Problems in Education: Front-Line Veterans on Their Combat Experience." *USSR Report: Military Affairs,* no. 1638 (7 December 1981):1—3. JPRS 79602. Translated by the Foreign Broadcast Information Service from the Russian article in *Znamenosets* [Standard-bearer], August 1981.

──── . "The Transbaikal Troops in the Hills of Manchuria." Translated under contract by the U.S. government from the Russian article in *Voyenno-Istoricheskiy Zhurnal* [Military history journal], August 1971, pp. 67—74.

Lukin, M. "In the Vyaz'ma Operation." *USSR Report: Military Affairs,* no. 1643 (7 January 1982):35—45. JPRS 79812. Translated by the Foreign Broadcast Information Service from the Russian article in *Voyenno-Istoricheskiy Zhurnal* [Military history journal], September 1981.

Mellenthin, Friedrich Wilhelm von. *Panzer Battles.* Translated by H. Betzler. New York: Ballantine Books, 1971.

Meretskov, Kirill Afanas'evich. *Serving the People.* Translated from the Russian by David Fidlon. Moscow: Progress Publishers, 1971.

Milovanov, P. "Crossing the Dnieper." *Military Review* 24 (June 1944):111—13. Translated from a Russian article in *Krasnaya Zvezda* [Red Star], 17 November 1943.

Moskalenko, K. "Offensive from Lutezh Bridgehead." *Soviet Military Review,* September 1966, pp. 41—44.

"Night Combat." *Military Review* 27 (February 1948):80—83. Translated and digested from an article in *Revista de la Oficialida de Complemento, Apendice de la Revista Ejercito* (Spain), May 1947.

Night Fighting. 2d ed. London: William Clowes and Sons, 1893. Photocopy of published pamphlet containing translation of article from *Svoennei Sbornik* [Russian military magazine], December 1885. CARL 355.422 S968n2.

Panov, V. "The Great Patriotic War and Postwar Period." *USSR Report: Military Affairs,* no. 1557 (16 January 1981):61—69. JPRS 77187. Translated by the Foreign Broadcast Information Service from the Russian article in *Voyenno-Istoricheskiy Zhurnal* [Military history journal], October 1980.

Pechenenko, S. "An Army Offensive Operation Under Conditions of the Far Eastern Theater of Military Operations." *Voyenno-Istoricheskiy Zhurnal* [Military history journal], August 1978, pp. 42—49. Translated under contract by the U.S. government.

"Peculiarities of Russian Warfare." Rev. ed. Mimeographed. U.S. Army, Historical Division, June 1949. MS T-22. CARL N16276. This document was published as U.S. Department of the Army Pamphlet no. 20—230, *Russian Combat Methods in World War II,* in June 1953 and has been reprinted.

People's Commissariat of Defense. "Infantry Tactical Manual of the Red Army." 1942. Mimeographed. Translated by the AC of S, G-2, GSUSA, 1951. CARL R16582.119.

Popov, A. "Reconnaissance in Strength." *Soviet Military Review,* March 1979, pp. 39—41.

"Red Army Field Service Regulations, 1942." Mimeographed. Translated from the Russian under the direction of the Chief of the General Staff, Canada. Ottawa, July 1944. CARL N15488A.

"Red Army Field Service Regulation, 1944." Mimeographed. Translated by the AC of S, G-2, Department of the Army, 1952. CARL N15488B.

Ribakov, Peter. "Soviet Night Attacks: Tanks." *The Cavalry Journal* 54 (May—June 1945):65—69.

Sazhin, A. "Breakthrough of a Fortified Region of the Enemy." Translated from *Voyennyi Vestnik* [Military Herald], 1944.

Schmidt, Paul Karl [Carell, Paul]. *Scorched Earth: The Russian-German War, 1943—1944.* New York: Ballantine Books, 1973.

Shishkin, S. "The Vitebsk Operation." *Military Review* 25 (July 1945):93—97. Translated from a Russian article in *Krasnaya Zvezda* [Red Star], 25 October 1944.

Shtemenko, Sergei Matveevich. "General Staff During the War." *Soviet Military Review,* September 1974, pp. 59—61.

_____. *The Soviet General Staff at War (1941—1945).* Translated from the Russian by Robert Daglish. Moscow: Progress Publishers, 1970.

Shutov, Z. "Night Operations." *Soviet Military Review,* September 1981, pp. 34—36.

Smith, Gorman C. "Division Night Attack Doctrine." Master's thesis, U.S. Army Command and General Staff College, 1964.
Sokolsky, Captain. "Night Raid on the Village of Khotomlya." *Military Review* 24 (June 1944):93—95. Translated from *Voyennyi Vestnik* [Military Herald], June 1943.
Sukhinin, Yo. "Combat Action of Rifle Divisions at Night." Translated by Lt. Col. David M. Glantz from the Russian article in *Voyenno-Istoricheskiy Zhurnal* [Military history journal], December 1977.
Sukhorukov, D. "Conclusions from the Experience of Airborne Landings in World War II." *USSR Report: Military Affairs*, no. 1627 (16 October 1981):71—79. JPRS 79225. Translated by the Foreign Broadcast Information Service from the Russian article in *Voyenno-Istoricheskiy Zhurnal* [Military history journal], July 1981.
Tretyak, I. "The Commander's Creative Activity." *USSR Report: Military Affairs*, no. 1587 (4 May 1981):37—40. JPRS 77987. Reprint from *Soviet Military Review*, August 1980.
Tsygankov, N. "Certain Features of Combat Operations of the 5th Army in the Harbin-Kirin Operation." Translated under contract by the U.S. government from the Russian article in *Voyenno-Istoricheskiy Zhurnal* [Military history journal], August 1975.
Tully, Andrew. *Berlin, Story of a Battle*. 1963. Reprint. Westport, CT: Greenwood Press, 1977.
Vasilevsky, A. "Second World War: Route of the Kwantung Army." *USSR Report: Military Affairs*, no. 1587 (4 May 1981):16—26. JPRS 77987. Reprinted from *Soviet Military Review*, special supplement, August 1980.
Werth, Alexander. *Russia at War, 1941—1945*. New York: E. P. Dutton and Co., 1964.
Yezhakov, Vasily. "The Berlin Operation." *Soviet Military Review*, April 1975, pp. 42—45.
Young, W. R. "Russian Strategy and Tactics." *Military Review* 24 (March 1945):120—22. Digested from an article in *The Fighting Forces* (Great Britain), 1944.
Zakharov, M. V. *Finale*. Translated by David Skvirsky. Moscow: Progress Publishers, 1972.
Zhukov, Georgii Konstantinovich. *Marshal Zhukov's Greatest Battles*. Translated from the Russian by Theodore Shabad. New York: Harper & Row, 1969.
Zvenzlovsky, A. "Night Attack." *Soviet Military Review*, May 1973, pp. 50—52.

STUDIES IN PROGRESS

The Soviet Strategic Offensive in Manchuria, August 1945: Overview and Cases

●

Defending the Driniumor: Covering Force Operations in New Guinea, 1943

●

U.S. Chemical Warfare Experience in World War I

●

Special Units: Rangers in World War II

●

Counterattack on the Naktong: Light Infantry Operations in Korea, 1950—51

●

Anglo-French Military Cooperation, March 1939—June 1940

●

Armored Combat in World War II: Arracourt

●

Evolution of Close Air Doctrine, 1940—80

●

Combat Operations in the Deep Desert: The LRDG

●

Stand Fast: German Defensive Doctrine in World War II

●

Combined Arms Doctrine in the 20th Century

●

Rapid Deployment Logistics, Lebanon, 1958

●

Operations of Large Formations: The Corps

●

Tactics and Doctrine in Imperial Russia

●

Postwar and Prewar Armies: How We Think About War

☆ U.S. GOVERNMENT PRINTING OFFICE 1988—554-001/82056

www.ingramcontent.com/pod-product-compliance
Lightning Source LLC
Chambersburg PA
CBHW081328040426
42453CB00013B/2334